Bob, Hope you Enjoy the book! [signature]

GOTHAM
BASEBALL

NEW YORK'S
ALL-TIME TEAM

MARK C. HEALEY

FOREWORD BY MARTY APPEL

ILLUSTRATIONS BY JOHN PENNISI
UNIFORM DESIGNS BY TODD RADOM

THE
History
PRESS

Published by The History Press
Charleston, SC
www.historypress.com

Front cover: design by Todd Radom.
Back cover, left to right: photo by Bill Menzel; Baseball Hall of Fame; Baseball Hall of Fame; Baseball Hall of Fame.

First published 2020

Manufactured in the United States

ISBN 9781467141635

Library of Congress Control Number: 2019956030

For Mom, you left us before this book was finished,
but I know you are proud of your baby boy.

For Cailin, my forever love.

For Julia, Jack and Jessica, best lineup ever.

For Dad, you gave me the love of the game.

CONTENTS

Foreword, by Marty Appel   7
Acknowledgements   11

1. From My Stoop to Cooperstown:
   The Story of *Gotham Baseball*   15
2. Putting the Team Together   31
3. Monte Irvin   36
4. Willie Mays   45
5. Babe Ruth   60
6. Christy Mathewson   73
7. Whitey Ford   79
8. Tom Seaver   87
9. Carl Hubbell   99
10. Dazzy Vance   104
11. Mike Piazza   112
12. Lou Gehrig   123
13. Jackie Robinson   132
14. Derek Jeter   141
15. David Wright   149
16. Mariano Rivera   157
17. Joe Torre   167
18. Ed Barrow   176
19. Joan Payson   182

Bibliography   189
About the Author   192

FOREWORD

All of Mark Healey's choices in this book are wrong.

There, I said it.

I said it because as I read the book I thought of the great sports columnist and author, the late Leonard Koppett, the smartest person I ever knew. Lenny liked to enter a room and say, "What are we talking about?…I disagree."

And sure enough, he was brilliant enough to take either side of an argument and win the day with his logic. If you said, "Lincoln was a pretty good president," Lenny could convince you otherwise. Or vice versa. He was brilliant.

So, I was thinking of Kop as I reviewed Mark's choices, thinking how much he would love to participate in, or create, a good debate…and then I reminded myself, "that, my friend, is the fun of sports." And this book accomplishes it.

This business of choosing "my guy or your guy" surely goes back to childhood debates on the sidewalks of New York, when Yankee fans and Giant fans would argue Lou Gehrig or Bill Terry as the best first baseman in town. In fact, in the early 1920s, fans were still putting Hal Chase, the notorious New York Highlanders' first baseman, in the discussion. He may have thrown a game now and then, but he had his supporters. He was handsome and had a swashbuckling style that connected with fans attracted by players with a touch of the notorious. The bad boys.

In my childhood, the Brooklyn Dodgers finally got good, and the argument covering center field went three ways: the Dodgers' Duke Snider, the Yankees' Mickey Mantle or the Giants' Willie Mays. Oh, how those debates mattered, and how they tested one's abilities at argumentation and debate, qualities that would stay with a person for the rest of their life. That one was the true test of fan loyalty.

Casey Stengel said, "I'd like to have all three." Now, that would have been a platoon!

Eventually, Duke dropped back in the argument, and we were left with Mantle vs. Mays. And finally, in 1995, it was Mantle who settled it by telling the audience at the annual New York Baseball Writers Association dinner, "Willie was the best of us." (Koppett was there, in the ballroom of the Sheraton Centre Hotel, but he did not rise to disagree. Disappointing.)

Those Yankee-Dodger seasons of the '50s were wonderful years for debating not only the center fielders, but also the catchers (Yogi Berra vs. Roy Campanella, three MVPs for each) and the shortstops (Phil Rizzuto vs. Pee Wee Reese).

And then, in 2001, I was working with Whitey Ford on a book (written with Phil Pepe) in which he chose the best Yankees of all time. Without hesitation, he named Derek Jeter over his longtime teammate Rizzuto. I was a little shocked; after all, he and Rizzuto had been friends for more than half a century. Jeter had only completed five seasons by then.

"Oh, it's Jeter," said Ford. "He does everything better than Phil except bunt. Rizzuto knows it's true."

Speaking of Jeter, I had long ago been taught to observe baseball as though it was unfolding history. One didn't need to wait years to make judgments or celebrate milestones. That was why there came a point when I would tap a friend on the shoulder and point to Jeter at short, Alex Rodriguez at third and Robinson Cano at second and say, "Look at that...you might be seeing the best third baseman, shortstop and second baseman in Yankee history all together at once, even with all the great players who have come before them."

Mark Teixeira at first base was pretty good, too, but now we're talking Gehrig, of course. Or Chase, if you were more than one hundred years old.

I was especially pleased to see Monte Irvin selected for left field. Monte doesn't get enough recognition today. I was proud of our being genuine friends—not someone whom I enjoyed going to lunch with because he was a Hall of Famer, but just because he was such good company. He was, in that sense, a regular guy with no airs, no sense of entitlement, no one looking for special courtesies.

And the truth is, he could well have been "the first"—he could have been Jackie Robinson. And, oh boy, to hear others tell it, what a ballplayer he was. He was maybe the best athlete to ever come out of New Jersey. (I hope that sounds like the compliment I intended it to be.) He did not get to the major leagues until he was thirty, and although he had fine seasons—third in MVP voting in 1951—most fans suspected that he must have really been something to see when he was in his twenties. Of that, Major League Baseball fans were robbed.

So, one day I just happened to ask this extremely modest man, "Who would you compare yourself to when you were at your prime, say in the early '40s, before the war. Were you like Willie Stargell? George Foster? Fred Lynn?"

He answered without hesitation. "Oh, DiMaggio," he said as he sprinkled salt on his fries. You could tell he meant it and that he'd always felt it, and as long as someone asked, he could give them an honest answer. DiMaggio.

I never looked at Monte the same after that. He was still this wonderful friend and great companion, but…he was as good as DiMaggio. I had no reason to doubt it, none at all. And when people talk about the color line before Jackie Robinson, I think of that and of how we baseball fans, those who have no color distinctions in watching the game, were deprived of having another DiMaggio in the game.

I'm glad he gets his just due here.

Another one I'm glad gets a shout-out is Christy Mathewson.

Had Mark written this book in 1910, Matty would have made the list, and had he and his heirs then updated it every ten years, Matty would have been in every edition. To last this long in the circuit of public opinion is a remarkable thing, because the natural aging process of the sport tends to vacuum up achievements.

For instance, if you led the league in something in year one—1876—you also held the all-time record. In year two, 1877, some of those records fell. By 1900, a whole bunch of them had fallen. By 2019, imagine how hard it would be to break a record that stood for over nearly a century and a half. That's why most statistical achievements today generally begin with "the best since.…"

New York has had some amazing ballplayers, but what a treat it must have been to go to the old Polo Grounds and watch Matty with his fadeaway. Mathewson was a control pitcher whose records today are hard to fathom. How do they even translate to the modern game? Imagine if you had Mathewson on your staff and you pitched him every fifth day and regularly pulled him after one hundred pitches to let the bullpen finish up. Unthinkable.

And I see Mark likes Mike Piazza behind the plate. I was all set to argue that it's neither Yogi Berra nor Roy Campanella, because Bill Dickey was better, but you've gone and picked Piazza.

Oh, this is going to get people talking. Which is, as we said, the very point. Readers, have at it. This is a lot of fun.

—Marty Appel

ACKNOWLEDGEMENTS

I t's fitting that a book written about Gotham's greatest was the product of the collaboration of so many people. I want to thank everyone who made it possible. But first, I have to say this.

I lost my mom, Marie, on November 21, 2018.

As I mention in chapter 1, she was the reason I started *Gotham Baseball*. When I got my book deal, she was the first person I called. It breaks my heart that she never got to see the finished product. Thankfully, my dad, who taught me the love of the game and has been my biggest fan, is still here and going strong.

For my amazing wife, Cailin, and my kids, Julia, Jack and Jessica, who selflessly allowed me to concentrate on this project for the last year-plus. I couldn't have done this without their support.

To John Pennisi, Todd Radom and Bill Menzel, for your friendship and for sharing your incredible gifts. This isn't a book without you.

Marty Appel's foreword might be the best-written section of this book, but I can handle that. He's been a great friend and mentor for many years.

To my cousin Paul Greco, who helped *Gotham Baseball* when it was needed most and whose belief in the project and in me personally will never be forgotten.

To Gene Berardelli, who helped save *Gotham Baseball* more than once. His friendship and counsel are invaluable.

Matt Cerrone, for his longtime friendship, advice, generosity and loyalty. Without his help, one of the most important chapters in this book doesn't get written.

Acknowledgements

To Keith Blacknick, Dan Twohig and the rest of the crew at the Queens Baseball Convention for all of the work you do.

To Brian Wright, who had no reason to assist me in helping this book published but did so anyway.

To Anna Gottlieb, who helped make sure my book proposal was ready for prime time.

To Michelle Moran, who took time out of her insanely busy life to share her expertise.

To J. Banks Smither at Arcadia Publishing/The History Press, for believing in the project and pushing it forward.

To *The Wave*'s publisher Walter Sanchez and his family, who didn't just allow me the time to work on this book but encouraged me as well.

To the staff at *The Wave*, past and present, especially Paula DiGioia, for her reimagination of *Gotham Baseball*'s print identity.

To Tom Seaver, David Wright, Howie Rose, Ron Darling, Joe Torre, Mariano Rivera, Mike Piazza, Derek Jeter, Joe Girardi, Jim Duquette, Billy Staples, Bob Hendrick, Jonathan Eig, Robert Murphy, James S. Hirsch, Bill Jenkinson, Lee Lowenfish, Mike Vaccaro, Ed Coleman, Michael Shapiro, Debra Hazel, Mike Lynch, Mathew Brownstein and Dave Studeman, who all made the time to be interviewed by me over the years. Your words certainly helped this book immensely.

To Buck O'Neil, Gary Carter and Ray Robinson. May you all rest in peace. I'm lucky to have spent time with each of you during my journey.

To Shaun Clancy, for hosting my book launch at his wonderful pub, Foley's NY, and for many years of friendship.

To Rick Cerrone, for always treating *Gotham Baseball* with respect.

To Patrick Teale, for helping me navigate my way through the early years.

To Brian Orefice and all of the folks at AP MegaSports, who gave me the best training I could have asked for. There's a special place in my heart for all of you.

To all of the great folks who have contributed over the years to *Gotham Baseball*: Marty Appel, Art Shamsky, John Sickles, Greg Prince, Karen Cousino, Joseph M. Lara, Stacey Lavender, Bryan Hoch, Joe McDonald, Chip Armonaitis, Faith Armonaitis, Ed Shakespeare, Cecilia Tan, Linda Berardelli, Ken "Trolley" Schlapp, William Cummings, Butch Moran, Pete Borellio, Edward Leos, John Buro, Joe Pietaro, Aaron Ross, Al Cohn, Elio Velez, David Lippman, Nicole Roberge, Christina Santucci, Howard Megdal, Chris Vaccaro, Dmitri Cavalli, Michael Dittelman, Robert M. Narvaez, Scott Dratell, Peter Sweeney, Martin Dolitski, John Pellino, Rich

Morris, Josh Landsburg, Mark Leff, Michael O'Kane, Joe Janish, Bart Alexander, Chris Villano, Lenny Melnick, Brian Jeske, Todd Krull, Kristin Krafft, Ralph Lee, Ann Bare, Jim Ferme, Ellen Volpe, Jim McQueen, Joe Lara, Stacey Lavender, Paul Francis Sullivan, Rob Shaw, Gary Armida, Robert Pimpsner, John MacKinade, Karen Sabatini, Matt Dahlgren, Adriana Soler-Kozarowitzsky, Jessica Quiroli, Shai Kushner, Jerry Milani, Michael Dowd, Jim Paguaga, Arnie Mazer, Matt Sherman, Stephen Hanks, Joe Favorito and John Sheridan.

I

FROM MY STOOP TO COOPERSTOWN

THE STORY OF *GOTHAM BASEBALL*

If opportunity doesn't knock, build a door.
—*Milton Berle*

L ife is a journey" is a popular cliché, but as author Terry Pratchett once wrote, "the reason that clichés become clichés is that they are the hammers and screwdrivers in the toolbox of communication."

In this case, the journey is my professional career. Perhaps the best way to describe it? My life has always been a sitcom, and God never changes the channel.

Thankfully, *Gotham Baseball* has been a huge part of the show.

I grew up in the Flatbush section of Brooklyn, a great place to be a kid. It was the 1970s, and on most days, me and my friends—Tommy "Sully" Sullivan, Rob Smith, Erik Neilis, Bobby Foronjy, Andy Hooven and Evan Brown—would gather on one of the stoops on East 39th Street and constantly argue about sports, mostly baseball.

The debates usually revolved around whose favorite players were better, whose teams had a shot at the playoffs and so on. It was our sports radio, our Twitter, and it was glorious.

The summer of 1977 was a rough one, however, as the inexplicable trade of Tom Seaver left us Mets fans without our one lynchpin, the best pitcher in town. (It was also the summer Elvis Presley died. Being a huge Elvis fan, it was a pretty tough double-whammy.)

We all followed the Dick Young/Jack Lang battle over Seaver in the *Daily News*, because every day, one of us would go to Joe's candy store, get the newspapers and talk about the stories we read. We never thought Seaver would get traded.

When he did, well, that sucked.

Still, I tried to root for the guys the Mets got back in the deal: Pat Zachry, Doug Flynn, Steve Henderson and Dan Norman.

I especially liked Henderson and the way he twirled his bat when he was getting ready to hit. I copied it all the time. Sadly, the 1977 Mets would finish in sixth place in the NL East and would do so for the next three seasons. Meantime, the Yankees would be winning World Series titles and taking over the back pages for the next several years as George Steinbrenner, Billy Martin and Reggie Jackson waged their private little wars for all to see.

But as bad as the Mets were all those years, we still did our thing on the stoop every day; we'd talk about the previous night's game, then we'd play Wiffle ball—all the time. I vividly remember arguing with my buddy Rob Smith because I wanted to "be" Lee Mazzilli as we played—and he felt that, since he was the better hitter, he should get to "be" Maz.

"But I look more like him, I'm even wearing the wristband on my forearm!" was my reply.

We also had a tremendous rivalry with the East 38th Street guys, led by Chris O' Donnell (Sully's cousin) and Jimmy Gillespie. Mike Hennigan from East 40th Street was another pal, as was Kevin Jamin and his brother Mark. (They lived on Farragut Road.)

I remember the day that Yankee captain Thurman Munson died, and the look on the faces of my friends Erik and Bobby—huge Yankee fans—when we heard the news.

Back then, I hated the Yankees—a trait handed down by my dad, Ronnie, who was a Brooklyn Dodgers fan. But I loved Munson as a player. It was a very sad day.

At the end of the day, no matter who we rooted for, we were fans. Real fans.

I can't speak for other neighborhoods or other fans of our era, but the boys on East 39th Street were not of the casual variety, as it was not an environment for front-runners. You had to be legit. You had to make your case with real numbers and intimate knowledge of the subject at hand. To us, a real fan not only knew what was happening now but also had to know the history of the team they rooted for, know the prospects coming up in the system, etcetera. Otherwise, you'd be labeled a front-runner and never live it down.

In retrospect, it was a great training ground for a journalist. Combine that with a passion for baseball, and I was doing real-time research every day about the game I loved without even realizing it. The funny thing is, I never thought I would make money writing about it.

As the years passed, it was becoming clear that it was time to leave Flatbush. I had been mugged twice; two guys tried to steal my brand-new bike, and when I wouldn't get off, one of them broke my finger with a pair of pliers. Thank goodness the gas station attendant was right there and chased them off with a tire iron.

The other time was just a few doors down from my house. Some guys flashed a knife, but they ran after I yelled out for my dad.

I know, it could have been a lot worse, but it still scared the crap out of me.

Then, our house was robbed. My dad, who worked for the New York City Department of Sanitation, and my mom, who was a nurse, told my two brothers and my sister, "That's it, we're moving."

I had just finished my freshman year at Xaverian High School in Brooklyn (1983) and had really bonded with all the guys I had hung out with that year: Brian Duffy, Billy Casey, Kevin ("Razor") McCarthy, Brian Lynn, Danny Brogan and Damon Michalopoulos. Of course, my pal Sully was the glue that brought us all together.

I'm happy to say that most of the guys I grew up with are still in my life, and that is a rare gift that keeps on giving.

But part of me wanted a fresh start. I had been bullied by a lot of the older kids in Flatbush. I wore glasses, and because of playing sports, I often broke them and had to wear tape on them until my parents could afford new ones. The older kids in the neighborhood called me "Myron," and for a few years, while other kids loved seeing the snow, I dreaded the walk home from school. Getting hit in the face with a snowball might be funny in the movies, but it sucked in real life.

It didn't get any better in high school. "Myron" became "Spaz" (from the movie *Meatballs*, which features a kid with tape on his glasses), and on Freshman Field Day, the whole gym was chanting "Spaz! Spaz! Spaz!" I wanted to cry, I wanted to run away, but you know what? They might have been calling me Spaz, but they were cheering, not throwing stuff at me. So, I smiled, ran onto the court, jumped up and slapped the backboard on my way into the gym and just rolled with it.

A week or so later, I ran for student government, wanting to be freshman representative. I won in a landslide. Sully and the CYO boys always had my back, and it made everything else kind of fade away.

My parents were concerned most about my transition; there was talk about me staying with Sully's parents (they had moved to Rockaway Beach, another sign of things to come) during the week to stay in Xaverian. But in the end, we left Brooklyn in the summer of 1984, and my family settled in Flushing, Queens, home of my Mets.

I chose Holy Cross High School, a much smaller school, which I think really helped me acclimate to totally new surroundings. I auditioned for *Joseph and the Amazing Technicolor Dreamcoat*, intent on playing the Pharaoh, who is basically Elvis. I had been imitating Elvis for years, and figured, hey, I could do that and maybe meet some girls. Holy Cross was a boys-only school back in 1983–84.

Being in school musicals changed everything for me. I made lots of friends, and I went from being a discipline problem to being a solid citizen.

During my senior year, I hosted *The Mark Healey Sports Machine*, a short "radio show" over the P.A. system every morning. It was a quick recap of the weekend's sports action. Later that year, I was asked to appear on 1050 WHN-AM's *In the Public Interest*. I was also the president of the speech and debate team, getting to the finals of the New York State Forensics League championships. The acting was fun, and I was good at it, but sports was where I wanted to be.

But was it the right path?

When I was about twelve or thirteen, I was pretty fast. I could play the outfield with ease, and despite my poor eyesight, I could hit pretty well. So, when my Uncle George "Georgie" Greco told me, "Kid, you're going to be a great sportscaster," I was a little hurt—at first.

Uncle Georgie was one of my favorite uncles, so I took it for what it was, which was that he got a kick out of the fact that this little kid could talk sports with the rest of my older relatives.

So, as a freshman at Queens College in 1986—the year the Mets won the World Series—I majored in communications, hoping to break into baseball play-by-play by the time I graduated. I didn't really have any guidance here; I was just trying to follow a game plan. As each semester went by, it seemed that play-by-play was a pipe dream, and I started to think that the stage and screen was my true calling. I had been in a few plays in college and was signed by an agent after an Actor's Equity Showcase performance in an Off-Broadway show called *Custody*.

I took that as a sign and moved to Hollywood with my good friend Chris Cardona.

Oh, silly boy, what were you thinking?

It was 1992. All that happened in Los Angeles that summer was the Rodney King riots, a few earthquakes and me being robbed at gunpoint at a bus stop at Fairfax Avenue. I did manage to do some stand-up comedy at the Comedy Store and make some lifelong friends like Tommy Carano and Trevor Downs. But I was back in New York City by 1993.

I was a broken man.

But in 1989, I had met the woman of my dreams, Cailin Moran, who said she'd wait for me when I headed out west. She was the one who put me back together.

I tried to give acting one more try, but, while I had talent, I didn't care for the constant rejection or the lifestyle.

Working in sports media would not be much easier, but once I made up my mind, that was it.

I attended the Connecticut School of Broadcasting in 1994, and with the help of a classmate, Frank Begley, I secured an internship at WFAN Sports Radio.

WFAN was at the height of its powers in 1995, and part of my job was to assist the *Imus in the Morning* show. There, I met Mike Breen, who then was Don Imus's sports guy. One day, Mike admired the Brooklyn Dodgers jersey I was wearing, and we struck up a conversation. The next day, I asked him to listen to my demo tape.

He didn't just listen to my tape, he sat me down and gave me great advice on how to make a better demo.

Mike, who's now the lead play-by-play man for the NBA on ABC and for the Knicks on MSG Network, was instrumental in my being hired for my first professional broadcasting job in 1996, as the producer of the new morning drive news program at Stamford, Connecticut's AM station WSTC.

The name of the show was *Fairfield County NewsRadio*, and the hosts were Michele Donofrio and Bill Shepard. Michele and Bill were incredibly supportive of their new producer, who knew absolutely nothing about Stamford, Fairfield County, Connecticut or, really, how to produce a radio show. They patiently showed me the ropes, and what I lacked in ability, I made up for with effort.

The other person I shared the early morning newsroom with was WSTC sportscaster Bill Hall. This generous man recognized my passion for sports and started to find ways to put me on the air immediately. Other people at the station heard me on the air and started to use me as voice-over talent or for news reports.

That was the summer the Mets fired manager Dallas Green and hired Stamford's favorite son, Bobby Valentine, to be the manager. That was fortuitous for several reasons. First, it allowed me to do some on-air spots about the Mets, and second, I had been a Bobby V fan since he appeared as a Mets player at Xaverian High School's father-son sports night when I was a kid.

Another memorable moment was during the 1996 World Series. The Yankees were down two games to none to the Atlanta Braves and were headed to Atlanta. Michele and Bill brought me into the studio and asked me on the air if the Yankees were done. "I'm not a Yankees fan, but I do think they can come back and win," I said. "The 1986 Mets did it, why not the Yankees?"

When the Yankees came back and won, it certainly didn't hurt my standing at the station. However, Commodore Media would wind up selling WSTC to Atlantic Star Media, and soon, like many other employees, I was out of a job.

A few months later, I was hired by John Wilson to run the evening/overnight news desk at WRKL-AM in Rockland County, and it was a great ride with some great people, like Anthony Guido, Jon Feld. Sean Adams, Scott Salotto, Marshall Stevenson, Pam Puso and Kyle Casey. But after a year of my personal and professional growth, WRKL was sold as well, this time to a company that changed the format to Polish-language broadcasting content.

Seriously.

Well, as my (good) luck would have it, after a week of being unemployed, I was hired by the Associated Press in June 1998 to work on the national baseball desk as an editorial assistant and dictationist. In short, I would communicate with sportswriters in different cities around the country, serve as a conduit between the writers and editors and then assist in finalizing the story for the sports wire. Most of the emphasis was on Major League Baseball, and I was given the job of writing the play-by-play account of the 1998 World Series.

I was in heaven.

For the next few years, I was a pretty happy guy. My first child, Julia, was born in 1999.

Then, in 2000, I found out that there was a baseball team coming to Brooklyn, and I knew I had to be a part of it.

The Brooklyn Cyclones were going to be the Single-A affiliate for the Mets in 2001, and I knew it would be a great opportunity. I wanted to be a part of it, desperately.

It just so happened that one of my coworkers, Pete Catapano, was the managing editor of the *Brooklyn Skyline* newspaper, a weekly. I asked him if the paper was going to be covering the team, and he said it would be. When I offered him my services, he said they already had someone on the staff he was planning on using to cover the games.

"Pete, there's no way he is as good as I am. Hell, I will do it for free," I said. He replied that he would think about it, and he did. Soon after, gave me the gig. He also paid me a solid freelance fee, I should add.

It would be one of the most memorable summers of my life. Being on a real baseball beat was incredibly educational and rewarding. Getting to spend time with players Brett Kay, Blake McGinley and future MLBers Angel Pagan, Mike Jacobs, Lenny DiNardo and Danny Garcia was a blast as well.

Just as the team was one game away from winning the New York Penn League title, terrorists attacked the World Trade Center and murdered thousands of innocent people. My wife was pregnant and was due any day. Nine days later, just moments after President George W. Bush addressed Congress and the nation, my son Jack was born.

I would cover the Cyclones for the next several years. Thanks to connections I made at the ballpark, I covered the Mets minor-league system for the then-official New York Mets magazine, *Mets Inside Pitch*, and its online partner, NYFansOnly.com. I also became a regular on-air contributor on the SportsNet New York weekly television show *Mets Weekly*. I was also working full-time at AP. Things were really busy, but they were pretty damn good.

Then, just like that, the ride got a little more interesting.

My daughter Jessica was born in the summer of 2004. Cailin and I had bought our first house and moved to Long Island, and AP moved as well, leaving its historic headquarters at 50 Rockefeller Center to go to 450 West 33rd Street, the former *New York Daily News* building.

By then, I was working in a department called "AP Megasports," which was the first national sports newsroom to be all-digital. It was a wonderfully hectic environment, filled with a cast of characters that would have occupied a season or two of *Barney Miller*. When I finally saw the new digs, I was ecstatic. We all had multiple-screen workstations, and we were much closer to Penn Station.

But just as we were just settling in, we found out that most of us were getting a pink slip.

Aug. 4, 2005—News Corporation and The Associated Press announced today that they have formed a joint venture named STATS, LLC to produce sports data and content. The joint venture will combine STATS Inc., the country's leading sports information and statistical analysis company, owned by News Corporation, and MegaSports, AP's multimedia sports service. Under the new agreement, News Corporation and AP will each own half of the joint venture. AP MegaSports is an online digital product that includes stories from the AP sports wire, AP sports photos, audio clips and schedules, and standings. It currently is sold to both AP members as well as commercial Web sites.

Under the new agreement, the MegaSports product will not change.

Well, the product did change, because half of the people creating the product didn't want to move to Chicago. That wasn't the most frustrating part. AP did little to nothing to retain most of us after the move.

The rumors had started years earlier. One had us moving to the West Coast. But when it didn't happen, most of us figured we'd be safe. I mean, there are people who have worked at AP for forty years, and we were the cutting edge of digital sports media.

So much for that.

When reality hit, many of us who weren't making the move inquired about other positions with AP Sports and were pretty much ignored. I'm not just talking about myself. There were other quality people (some I admit even more qualified than myself) similarly left out in the cold.

When I spoke to a union rep, he told me, "Sorry pal, we are sitting this one out." I asked why, and the rep shrugged his shoulders.

I'm pretty sure I knew the answer; many of the people in our department had never joined the union. There was no requirement to do so, so they got the benefit of union protection without paying any dues. Being the son of a Teamster, I had joined the union the first week I was hired in June 1998. So, yeah, I felt a little betrayed.

I was also powerless, so it was a bitter time for me, to say the least. Unlike most of the people in the department, I was married with three kids and a mortgage and was truly concerned about what I would do next.

The brass at AP wasn't going to fold us into AP Sports, and other departments were giving us the high hat.

I can't speak to everyone else's experience, but I felt like I had spent eight years at the biggest news agency in the world and I couldn't even get an interview for a similar position at a company I had worked my ass off for. So, I stuck around until they threw me out.

Thankfully, the new parent company, STATS LLC, understood what was at stake. It had asked some of us to stay through the transition, which took almost a year, and we actually got a nice severance package and bonus for staying on until January 2006.

But in April 2005, I had already begun building my own door.

Gotham Baseball started with one idea: to create a publication that covered the past, present and future of New York baseball.

Though I always credit my dad for giving me the love and foundation for baseball knowledge, it's my mom, Marie, who deserves credit for the birth of *Gotham Baseball*. Mom was always buying me books about baseball, but *100 Years of Major League Baseball: American and National Leagues, 1901–2000* was the trigger. The book did a wonderful job of chronicling MLB's history year by year, with illustrations and fun facts. I found myself reading a story about how Hall of Fame pitcher Jack Chesbro won 41 games in 1904 while pitching for the Yankees (then called the Highlanders) while still finding a way to lose the last game of the season to the Boston Red Sox and lose the pennant.

I thought to myself: Who the heck is Jack Chesbro? Is 41 wins in a season really the record? And how the heck did I not already know this?

At that moment, I realized that there should be a place where fans of all ages could read about all of their favorite baseball teams, whether Brooklyn Dodgers, New York Giants, New York Yankees or New York Mets. I also thought that there were few people who had the passion, knowledge and talent to do so, so I reached out to some folks who I thought could help me get this thing off the ground, and *Gotham Baseball* was born.

"The Past, Present, and Future of the New York Game" was our tagline, and we went full throttle with the concept. Our first issue was prospect-based, with No. 1 Mets prospect Yusmeiro Petit and Yankees top phenom Eric Duncan on the cover.

We were thrilled when Amazon.com's "Editor's Picks" named *Gotham Baseball* one of the best new magazines of 2005—the only sports magazine on the list.

The biggest thrill, though, was a call from Judith Wells.

I was standing in line at the post office, getting ready to mail out some magazines to new subscribers, when I got a call from Ms. Wells, who identified herself as the executive assistant to George Steinbrenner. "Mr. Steinbrenner was very impressed with your *Gotham Baseball* magazine," she said. "He asked that I contact you to see if it would be possible for you to send him a few more copies to share with his general partners."

I think I sent him about a hundred.

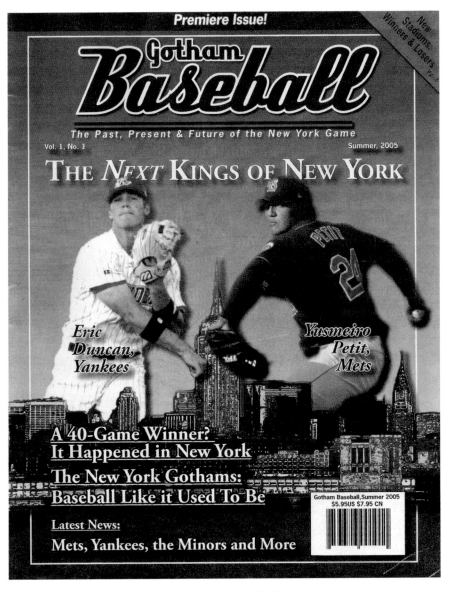

The first issue of *Gotham Baseball* magazine. *Author's collection.*

Weeks later, I received a congratulatory letter from Steinbrenner himself, in which he wrote, "I believe that New York can support a magazine such as yours and I wish you a great deal of success."

Ironically, this die-hard Mets fan was getting respect and congrats from the Yankees, thanks to people like former Yankee PR director Rick Cerrone (now the editor-in-chief at *Baseball Digest*). In truth, while Cerrone was with the Yankees, I was always treated like another member of the media, which is all I ever asked for.

The Mets—well, let's just say the relationship has always been a little more complicated.

Gotham Baseball's early success led to some turmoil behind the scenes, as the partnership I had built started to fray and egos collided.

My friend Gene Berardelli, whom I met during the Cyclones inaugural season of 2001, had become a friend and a close confidant. Given his standing as a practicing attorney, I asked him to get involved, and he was able to legally save *Gotham Baseball*—not once, but twice—from hostile takeovers.

In addition, my cousin Paul Greco—who soon built a reputation as a great fantasy sports expert and is now one of the top women's softball coaches in the great state of Texas—came on board as a partner. If not for these two guys, *Gotham Baseball* would have been a bitter memory.

So, we pushed forward. *Gotham Baseball* was now a credentialed media outlet. We covered the MLB winter meetings, as well as the Brooklyn Cyclones, Staten Island Yankees, Long Island Ducks, Mets and Yankees. We also covered local college baseball and even high school content.

In summer 2007, I rolled the dice on what was to be our biggest issue yet. It was our seventh issue, and we dedicated it to Mickey Mantle. I doubled the page count, commissioned the cover to be designed and illustrated by the wonderful John Pennisi and partnered with Mickey Mantle's Restaurant and the Mantle family to unveil the cover in our first-ever press conference.

It was the first time I'd work with Marty Appel, the former Yankee PR director, esteemed historian and best-selling author. Marty was doing PR for Mantle's, and one of my colleagues, Michael Dittelman, introduced us via email. It started a relationship that exists today, obviously. Marty opened up so many doors for us and has been someone I have confided in at the best and worst of times.

I had my stunning wife, Cailin, and my three little cuties unveil the cover, and Marty and several others who had attended the press conference loved it. The presser went so well that we got the go-ahead to launch a new podcast, *Live at Mickey Mantle's*, which was the first sports podcast at a live venue for the new platform BlogTalkRadio (BTR).

At that time, podcasts were still a new thing, but doing them from a live venue was something no one was doing. This intrigued BTR CEO Alan Levy, who even traveled to Mantle's for our first episode.

Illustrated by John Pennisi, the seventh edition of *Gotham Baseball* was dedicated to Mickey Mantle. *Author's collection.*

"BlogTalkRadio is proud to be able to provide a platform that allows citizen broadcasters like Gotham Baseball to produce high-quality shows from anywhere in the world. 'Live from Mickey Mantle's' is a demonstration of what BlogTalkRadio can do in the hands of enthusiastic business people," said Levy.

I still feel bad that he got a parking ticket during the broadcast. I've always been grateful to BTR for its help and have worked with them ever since.

Financial obstacles kept us from printing another magazine until the summer 2008 issue, "The City Game." It would turn out to be our last print issue. Printing costs were astronomical, so we tried something different. It was the first *Gotham Baseball* magazine also available online.

About a week later after its release, I received a letter from James L. Gates, the librarian of the National Baseball Hall of Fame and Museum in Cooperstown, New York: "A member of our public relations staff recently passed along two issues of your magazine....We believe this periodical would make a valuable addition to our library collection. The Library of the National Baseball Hall of Fame contains a comprehensive archive of material related to all aspects of our great national pastime and we would like to include your magazine."

New York Yankees

GEORGE M. STEINBRENNER III

YANKEE STADIUM
BRONX, NEW YORK 10451
TEL: (718) 293-4300

September 17, 2007

Mark C. Healey, Executive Editor
Gotham Baseball Magazine
PO Box 321
Lynbrook, New York 11563

Dear Mr. Healey:

Thank you for sending me so many copies of the Summer 2007 edition of your magazine *Gotham Baseball*. We distribute them to the employees and share the balance with guests visiting Legends Field. They are always a big hit with everyone who reads it.

I found the article on Mickey and Andy particularly interesting. I also enjoyed the story on Leo Durocher – it has been a while since his name has been mentioned in relation to the Cubs – glad you included him in this issue.

Thank you for your kind words with regard to the support and cooperation you received from the Yankee organization - let me know if you ever run into a problem. Marty Appel was a great PR Director and a great guy. Since leaving the Yankees he's done well for himself, which is a testament to his ability.

Thank you for thinking of me and I'm pleased that *Gotham Baseball* has been so successful for you.

Sincerely,

George M. Steinbrenner III

This letter, from Yankee principal owner George Steinbrenner, has been an inspiration for me for many years. *Author's collection.*

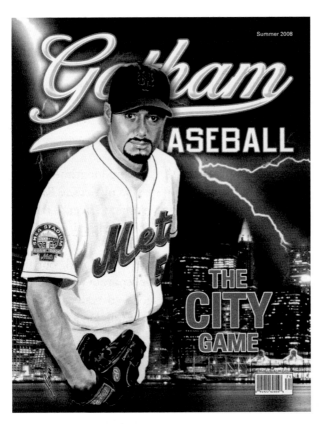

Left: The acquisition of Johan Santana was supposed to put the Mets in the playoffs in 2008. Instead, the team was eliminated on the last game ever at Shea Stadium on the last day of the regular season. *Author's collection*.

Below: "Sixty Summers" was a collaborative effort by the author and Stacy Lavender and was published in the fall 2011 issue of *Gotham Baseball* magazine. *Author's collection*.

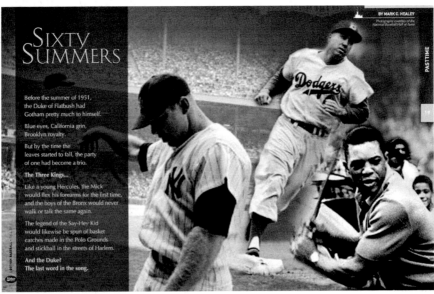

Wow. The Hall of Fame?

It was also around this time that Norman Jacobs, the owner of the legendary *Baseball Digest* magazine, and I entered into a licensing agreement to bring his classic magazine to the internet, with *Gotham Baseball* as the first of what would be a network of affiliates across the country.

A daily, live podcast, *Baseball Digest LIVE*, broadcast from Foley's NY in Manhattan, soon followed. Not long after that, *Baseball Digest Fantasy Baseball* debuted on SiriusXM in 2011.

Also in 2011, I was introduced to Joseph M. Lara by longtime friend Nick D'Arienzo, and he agreed that an all-digital version of *Gotham Baseball* magazine was a great idea. He brought in designer Stacy Lavender from BallyhooCentral.com, and we created four incredible digital issues of *Gotham Baseball*.

After four issues, the result was the same: critically acclaimed, but not enough revenue. Joe and I shook hands and went our separate ways.

I couldn't give up on *Gotham Baseball*, so I decided to concentrate on GothamBaseball.com. Helped by so many people, including Joe McDonald, Robert Pimpsner, Shai Kushner, Gary Armida, Jerry Milani and many others, I was able to keep *Gotham Baseball* alive and viable as a destination for great content.

Along the way, I also became managing editor, now editor-in-chief, of *The Wave* newspaper in Rockaway Beach, and I was working full-time for someone else for the first time in many years. The publisher graciously allowed me to start including *Gotham Baseball* content in the paper, and the response started to form a new idea in my mind.

The *Gotham Baseball* concept has always seemed to interest people, but my execution of it had fallen short. Then it hit me: why not write a *Gotham Baseball* book?

I've been a fan of baseball books my entire life, and my favorite as a little boy was *Baseball's Youngest Big Leaguers*, by John Devaney. I must have read that a thousand times. Other favorites were *The Boys of Summer* by Roger Kahn, Ed Linn's *Sandy Koufax* and Roger Angell's *The Summer Game*.

I spoke with several friends, who all seemed to think a book was a good idea. It wasn't until I spoke with longtime pal and media consultant Matt Cerrone that I really started to get excited about the idea.

I had dabbled with a "Field of Dreams" type of concept, but Marty Appel said, "Who's the bad guy?" and I didn't have an answer.

Finally, I decided that creating an all-time team might be the ticket. It was something I had come up with a few years earlier for a different project.

The All-Time Gotham Baseball Team ballot picked the best player from each team: New York Yankees, New York Mets, Brooklyn Dodgers and New York Giants. It was broken down by position (catcher, first base, second base, third base, shortstop, left field, center field, right field, right-handed starting pitcher, left-handed starting pitcher, closer, manager, general manager and owner), then distributed to several websites and other friends to share.

Thousands of people voted and posted on social media about the process. So, fast-forward to 2017. I thought to myself, I have this ballot, and there has never been a book about the best all-time team from New York.

So, it was "go time."

2

PUTTING THE TEAM TOGETHER

In a world of sports information coming at you from all directions, a go-to destination remains Gotham Baseball, *expertly piecing together the past and the present, and serving it up just as sports fans like it.*
—*Marty Appel*

I would be lying if I thought writing this book was going to be hard.

I mean, I founded *Gotham Baseball*, have been writing about sports for twenty-five years and crank out thousands of words a week. I've written about most—if not all—of the folks in this book, and I had the voting results from the ballot.

However, I still had to decide what kind of a book it would be. Visually, I knew I wanted it to be as representative of the *Gotham Baseball* brand as possible. That would mean it needed the artwork of John Pennisi and the photography of Bill Menzel.

I met John in 2005-ish after a colleague of mine, Aris Sakellaridis, told me about this friend of his who was a great artist. "You gotta see this guy's stuff, man." He showed me a book they had worked on together called *Yankees Retired Numbers*, which featured artwork by Pennisi and photos by Menzel.

I fell in love with their work from the very beginning. I would soon learn what great people they were, as well. John introduced me to Bill, and I'm proud to say that both aren't just folks who have contributed to *Gotham Baseball*, they've also been great friends and remain so to this day.

Since he came on board, Bill has provided incredible photos of the Mets and Yankees over the years and has always been there when we needed the tough-to-get shots of big moments.

As I mentioned in chapter 1, in 2007, the *Gotham Baseball* magazine's "7" edition was published. As it was our seventh issue ever, I decided to dedicate it to Mickey Mantle. John created a beautiful cover, reminiscent of the illustrated *Baseball Magazine* covers I had always wanted *Gotham Baseball* to emulate.

Needless to say, I was thrilled when John and Bill said they were on board for the book

So, as the band was getting back together, the next step would be a little more difficult. This would be the first book that selected the best players from among the ranks of the Mets, Yankees, Brooklyn Dodgers and New York baseball Giants. My mission was to find the best way to highlight the players and their respective teams while also creating a *Gotham Baseball*–branded squad.

I collaborated on the 2005 original logo, which was designed by Mike McGann. It appeared on our first three issues of the magazine. I liked it, but a year later, I decided to go with a completely new look.

I hired designer Karen Cousino to redesign the 2006 version. I wanted the new design to put more emphasis on "Gotham" and really wanted more of a baseball feel.

This time around, I wanted an element from every team in the design: the navy (Yankees), orange (Mets), the tail (Dodgers) and the *G* (similar to the 1951 Giants logo). Some of the elements were deliberately derivative, like the tail and the *G*, for obvious reasons, but I also wanted something original.

Karen did the actual design work, but I was more involved in the conceptual design this time around, and it was my wife, Cailin, who suggested the oval for the eventual primary logo.

At first, I was kind of dismissive when Cailin suggested it. Then, realizing she has a great eye for style, I asked Karen to put the new logo into an oval, and it looked fantastic.

The logo was great, the branding was strong and, over the years, my partner Gene Berardelli (who would create some great logos for *Gotham* as well) had some great ideas for what we called Gotham Gear, but none of those ideas ever got past a jpeg.

Then, my other partner, Paul Greco—also my cousin—came to New York for a visit and was bearing gifts: *Gotham Baseball* caps, tees and polo

In 2006, a new version of the *Gotham Baseball* logo was created. Concept by Mark Healey, design by Karen Cousino. *Author's collection.*

shirts featuring the 2006 logos. Though we weren't able to mass-produce the gear (we never had the money), the response was favorable.

So, ten years later, I decided that putting the players in a *Gotham Baseball* uniform would be a great way to bring the book together. Unorthodox? Perhaps. But it did help me focus and start the process.

I have always been a fan—and a critic—of uniform design. I've been a fan of Uni Watch's Paul Lukas and Phil Hecken for a long time, as well as Chris Creamer and his sportslogos.net website. My friend Mike Cesarano, whom I met in high school, is another huge fan of uniform design. He used to do a segment on my *Baseball Digest* podcast called "Across the UNI-verse."

Through them, I learned about artist Todd Radom. A brilliant designer and artist, his clients include MLB, the NFL, NBA and brands like Ice Cube's The Big 3. I had gotten to know Todd through social media, and we had several pleasant exchanges over the years. We finally got to meet in person at the first-ever Queens Baseball Convention in 2014, a Mets fan fest that I've been a part of since its inception.

A year later, Todd wrote to me, "We need to collaborate on your next venture, whatever that might be."

The new *Gotham Baseball* logo.
Design and photo by Todd Radom.

In 2016, when the process of this book started in earnest, I remembered what Todd had written to me, so I asked him if he had any interest in designing the Gotham Baseball uniform, and he said, "Sure, when do we start?"

Energizing wasn't the word.

After about a year of collaborating—and I use the term loosely, because Todd truly did all the work—the result was even more than I could have hoped for; he not only designed a beautiful uniform, he designed three, with home and road versions!

Each one has a specific feel, a historical identity (1950s, 1980s and 2017, or modern era) that built off the existing brand and advanced it in a way I never dreamed possible. The icing on the cake was the shoulder patch logo, which Todd felt was needed to enhance the overall brand.

I sent the designs to Pennisi, and he created the first portrait, of Monte Irvin, to go along with the sample chapter that would be part of the book proposal, which I started sending out to publishers in 2017.

In January 2018, I ran into my friend Brian Wright, the author of *Mets in 10s: Best and Worst of an Amazin' History*, who suggested I reach out to his publisher, Arcadia Publishing/The History Press.

It was a very generous gesture, and so I took him up on it. I didn't hear anything after several weeks, so I figured this was a dead end. As I had never written a book before, I decided to reach out to (serious name drop alert) international best-selling author Michelle Moran (*Nefertiti, Cleopatra's Daughter, Rebel Queen* and several more) for some advice. She's my wife's cousin, whom I met when I made my trek to Hollywood in the 1990s. We had stayed connected over the years.

Maybe there was something wrong with my proposal, so I asked her to take a look at it. She did a tremendous amount of work on it, and on the very day she sent it back, I received an email from J. Banks Smither at Arcadia Publishing/The History Press, who said his company was interested in the book!

"Wow, wow, wow!" wrote Michelle when I emailed her the news. "If this is the case, don't touch the proposal!" So I didn't change a thing. And here we are.

My only regret is that my mom passed away from cancer before this book would be published. I'm thankful she was alive long enough to know that someone had agreed to publish it. She was a force of nature and had beaten cancer twice before. "I can run circles around you, mister," she always used to say. This time, it would prove too much, even for her.

But as I write this, I'm smiling through tears at the memory of the joy in her voice when I called her to tell her the news that *Gotham Baseball: New York's All-Time Team* was going to be a real book.

So, here it is, and I sincerely hope you all enjoy it.

3

MONTE IRVIN

*Monte was the best all-around player I have ever seen. As great as he was in
1951, he was twice that good ten years earlier in the Negro Leagues.*
—Roy Campanella

onte Irvin flew like an Eagle and played like a Giant. But to all who
knew him or saw him perform, he was as great a man as he was a
ballplayer. A true gentleman. But the reason he's on this team is that,
in my opinion, he was the best left fielder to ever play in Gotham.

When I first set up the ballot for the left field category for the Gotham
Baseball all-time team, Irvin was an easy selection to be the New York Giants
representative. As I explain in chapter 2, each team that played in New York
was given a player on the ballot. For left field, the others were Zach Wheat
(Brooklyn), Kevin McReynolds (Mets) and Roy White (Yankees).

I was criticized by many for putting Roy White on the ballot ahead of
Hall of Fame Yankees like Dave Winfield and Rickey Henderson. But in
my mind, Roy was a lifetime Yankee who deserved to get a chance to be
voted in by the fans. If people wanted Winfield or Rickey on the team, they
had ample opportunity to write them in. They didn't, and after thousands
of votes, neither Winfield nor Henderson received more than 5 percent of
the vote.

Another surprising result was Irvin (37 percent) just narrowly beating
McReynolds (34 percent). I'll be honest, as a Mets fan, I liked McReynolds a
lot. Back when the Mets actually tried to get better after a successful season,

his trade to the Mets from San Diego for eventual MVP Kevin Mitchell (a valuable utility player in 1986) is often criticized now, but at the time, people loved getting the All-Star left fielder for a raw rookie.

McReynolds was a solid player for the Mets, and his four-year averages (.276 batting average, 26 home runs, 90 RBIs, 15 stolen bases) are not to be dismissed. But goodness, Irvin was majestic.

I once interviewed the legendary Buck O'Neil, and he described Monte Irvin as "one of the greatest ballplayers I'd ever seen." His face lit up when he described Irvin's game. "Look how great that young man did when he was thirty years old [in New York]," chuckled O'Neil. "When he was twenty? My goodness, he was a superstar."

Before his career was interrupted by World War II, Irvin certainly lived up to O'Neil's description. In 1940, his first full year for the Negro National League's Newark Eagles, the twenty-one-year-old Irvin's batting average was .351, his on-base percentage (OBP) was .370 and his slugging percentage (SLG) was .542, giving him an on-base plus slugging percentage (OPS) of .912.

The next season would be even better, as Irvin's slash line was .400/.431/.585 with a 1.015 OPS.

That kind of production, along with his superb fielding, speed and overall grace as a player and young man, soon made him special. For all his humility, though, Irvin also felt that the owners of the Eagles, Abe and Effa Manley, owed him a better salary.

In 1942, Irvin said he needed a $25 pay raise from his salary of $165 a month. The Manleys said they didn't have the finances to pay Irvin. So, like several players from the Negro Leagues—and the major leagues as well—Irvin accepted an offer from Mexican businessman Jorge Pasquel to play in the Mexican League.

Before Branch Rickey figured out that integrating baseball would be great business, Pasquel was actually the first person to prove that black and white ballplayers could play—and succeed—together.

John Virtue, the author of *South of the Color Barrier: How Jorge Pasquel and the Mexican Baseball League Pushed Baseball toward Racial Integration*, detailed Pasquel's offer to Irvin: a significant pay raise, plus a maid and an apartment.

After being rebuffed by the Manleys, Irvin headed south to join the Vera Cruz Blues. He got married, hit .398 and won the Triple Crown in the Mexican League, despite missing a third of the games. Unlike in the States, he also received equal treatment.

"For the first time in my life, I felt really free. You could go anywhere, go to any theater, do anything, eat in any restaurant, just like anybody else, and it was wonderful," Irvin told Peter Golenbock, author of *In the Country of Brooklyn*.

Then he got drafted into the U.S. Army, and everything changed for Monte Irvin. For most of the next three years, he wore a different uniform, and like many other MLB stars of that time, he may have lost the best of his playing years to World War II. It also cost him the role of being the first African American to break the color barrier in Major League Baseball.

In the spring of 1945, Rickey was searching the Negro Leagues to integrate organized baseball. He insisted that the candidate not only be a gifted ballplayer but also a military veteran with a college education. Rickey believed that those three qualifications were essential if the first African American player was to earn the respect of his white teammates as well as of the general public.

That same summer, Rickey reached out to Irvin to see if he wanted to become the first black man to play in the major leagues.

Rickey wasn't the only one who thought Irvin was the best candidate. "[In 1945], the Negro League owners and players took a poll that year asking which player would be the perfect representative to play in the major leagues," wrote Irvin in his autobiography, *Nice Guys Finish First*. "They said I was the one to do it, the perfect representative. I was easy to get along with, and I had some talent."

However, as he was being discharged from the army that summer, Irvin was suffering from an injury that affected his balance and sapped much of his strength. In his autobiography, Irvin referred to it as "a little nerve condition, an inner-ear imbalance....The doctor told me that my condition would probably improve when I got back home around friends and family and got busy."

So, Irvin, in his honesty and humility, declined, telling Rickey that he needed to get back into shape physically before he could sign any contract for the Brooklyn Dodgers and be "the first." Rickey wished him luck and told Irvin that he'd be keeping an eye on him. Jackie Robinson was later chosen by Rickey, and history was made.

In the meantime, Irvin went to winter ball to recuperate and rejoined the Eagles in 1946.

Now here's where things get interesting, because Rickey's search for talent didn't stop with Robinson. Soon after signing Robinson, Rickey signed both Roy Campanella and Don Newcombe from the Negro Leagues, and in 1946, both were playing for the Dodgers' Nashua farm team.

What about Irvin?

The narrative of St. Rickey is chronicled in many places, and while he did break the color barrier, let's just say I often find myself leaning toward the opinion of the late Ralph Kiner, Hall of Fame outfielder and longtime Mets broadcaster.

Kiner often contended—both on-air and to anyone who would ask—that Rickey's interest in the Negro League players was one of acquiring high value for less money, or "cheap labor." This doesn't make Rickey a bad guy, but we don't worship at the altar.

On his blog, author and baseball historian Joe Posnanski noted that "Rickey did not respect the Negro Leagues as a fully organized league and did not believe he needed to compensate Negro League owners for their players. Kansas City Monarchs owner J.L. Wilkinson let Jackie Robinson go without compensation because he believed it was the right thing, but he reportedly did resent Rickey for just taking his players as if the Monarchs were not a real team."

Also, while many praise Newark Eagles' co-owner Effa Manley for demanding hefty compensation for her players, her stubbornness also may have contributed to Irvin not reaching the majors sooner.

A case in point: In 1946, Irvin showed he was physically fit and able to perform, with an outstanding season and postseason for the eventual Negro League champion Eagles. Irvin hit a league-leading .404 with a .960 OPS. He also hit 3 home runs and batted .462 against the Kansas City Monarchs in the Negro World Series, whose pitching staff featured future Hall of Famers Hilton Smith and Satchel Paige.

Yet, still, no big-league offers for Irvin. Or were there? We'll never know.

In 1947, Jackie Robinson was leading the Dodgers to the National League pennant. Irvin was hitting .348 with a 1.161 OPS for Newark. There are many reports that there were teams interested in Irvin's services, but Manley's demands were considered too high for the twenty-eight-year-old.

However, Irvin's twenty-three-year-old teammate, Larry Doby, did get to the major leagues and became the first black player in the American League for Bill Veeck's Cleveland Indians.

On his blog *Did the Tribe Win Last Night?*, Vince Guerrieri writes that Veeck paid $10,000 for Doby's contract, and he made his major-league debut on July 5 of that year. Veeck paid Manley another $5,000 after Doby made the club. According to Guerrieri, Manley also offered Veeck the chance to sign Irvin, to which Veeck replied, "I think I'm going to have enough trouble bringing in one black. I'm afraid two might not be twice as complicated, but would instead be arithmetical, geometric."

In 1948, Rickey finally got around to signing Irvin to a minor-league contract, believing he was a free agent. At that point, the Negro Leagues were just about done, and the Manleys were trying to get as much money for their players as they could.

According to the book *Before the Glory: 20 Baseball Heroes Talk About Growing Up and Turning Hard Times into Home Runs*, coauthor Bill Staples said the Manleys had sold Irvin's contract to a Memphis dentist named W.H. Young for an undisclosed amount. Rickey bought the contract from the dentist for $10,000. However, there was a catch, as the dentist had arranged to split any money from a transaction for Irvin with the Manleys and then decided he didn't want to split Rickey's offer.

When Rickey learned he would have to pay the Manleys as much as an additional ten grand for Irvin, he balked, leaving Irvin once again in limbo.

Rickey's decision was the rival New York Giants' gain, as owner Horace Stoneham—after a push from his new manager, Leo Durocher—finally make good on a decade-old good intention by paying the asking price for Irvin.

In 1938, when Irvin was seventeen years old, he was a brilliant baseball player at East Orange High School in New Jersey. According to Posnanski, one of Irvin's teachers wrote to Stoneham. "We've got a player here," the teacher wrote, "you would not even believe."

Stoneham wasn't the first owner to flirt with the idea of signing black players to play in the majors. Former Giants manager John McGraw had long admired black players and often told others he wished he could have signed a few of them to help his club win. So, he sent scouts to see Irvin play. Posnanski writes that, years later, Irvin would ask Stoneham what the scouts said. "They told me," Stoneham said sadly, "that you were the next Joe DiMaggio."

In 1938, however, no one in baseball had the courage—or the leverage—to sign black players. "I only wish I had been braver than that," Stoneham would tell Irvin many years later.

While Stoneham was the one who finally gave the okay to sign Irvin, it was Durocher who deserves much of the credit for the Giants' decision to join the Dodgers and Indians in breaking the color line. Durocher was the manager of the Dodgers when Rickey signed Robinson, and he supported the idea of integration of the game from the get, famously telling Dodgers who refused to play with Robinson and signed a petition to that effect that they could "wipe their ass with it." Durocher's contention was that if one could help his team win, he would play.

Irvin's career with the Giants started in the minors. In sixty-three games in Jersey City, he hit .373 with 55 runs scored, 52 RBIs, 14 stolen bases and 32 extra-base hits. He didn't impress—or even play much—after he was called up in July, managing to hit just .224 in thirty-six games. (He did manage an impressive .366 OBP over that span, but no one really cared about OBP in 1949.)

Despite his strong year in the minors, Irvin couldn't seem to break into the everyday lineup in 1950, either, so he was sent back to Jersey City to start the year. Irvin didn't protest; he took it out on the baseball. In just eighteen games, he hit .510 and hit 10 home runs. Durocher knew it was time for Monte to do his thing in the Polo Grounds.

Playing in 110 games, Irvin hit .299 with a .392 OBP, hitting 15 home runs and driving in 66 runs. He also managed to compile a .889 OPS, all while playing several positions, including 59 games at first base, the only spot Durocher could finagle his bat into the lineup early in the season. He would play right field (30 games) and left field (20 games) and even one game at third base.

It was a pretty good season, but not up to the standard Irvin expected of himself. In 1951, he would finally get to show everyone in baseball— especially Branch Rickey, now toiling away in last place as the general manager of the Pirates—just what they were missing all of those years.

Irvin's season in 1951 was nothing short of amazing. He hit .312, with a .415 OBP and a .929 OPS, slamming 21 homers and driving in 121 runs, scoring 94 runs while striking out just 44 times in 558 at-bats.

Something else happened in 1951, as Durocher convinced Stoneham to promote a young center fielder hitting .477 from Triple-A Minneapolis to the big club. "Leo asked me to room with Willie Mays when he was called up in late May, and of course I was happy to do so," recalled Irvin. "I was supposed to show Willie the ropes and we spent a lot of time together off the field. We got along very well and have never said an unkind word to each other then or in all the years since."

Irvin's leadership proved to play a major factor not only in Mays's eventual Rookie of the Year performance; his steadiness and consistency also helped propel the team to the pennant, its first NL flag since 1937.

Sure, Leo was employing a sign-stealing operation at home—as told by Joshua Prager in his book *The Echoing Green*—which certainly helped tip the scales. But on September 5, the Giants started a fourteen-game

After joining the New York Giants in 1949, Monte Irvin finally got his chance to shine. *Photo by the Baseball Hall of Fame.*

road trip, trailing the Dodgers by six games. New York went 10-4 on the trip, whittling Brooklyn's lead to four games at the beginning of their final three-game homestand. Scoring precisely four runs each game, the Giants swept the Boston Braves at the Polo Grounds, which still left them two and a half games back with two games remaining in Philadelphia and two in Boston. They won all four, while the Dodgers lost four of their final seven (also all on the road) to end the scheduled season tied for first. Winning fourteen of the last eighteen road games was indispensable to catching the Dodgers. It should be mentioned that Irvin also played better on the road in 1951 across the board, including an OPS of .971 away from the Polo Grounds, compared to .884. During that September pennant push, Irvin also hit .336 with an OPS of 1.049, his best showing of any month that season.

Though the Giants would lose the World Series in six games to the New York Yankees, Irvin shined in the Fall Classic, batting .458 in 24 at-bats, including a steal of home.

The following spring, toward the end of spring training, Irvin broke an ankle while sliding into third base and wouldn't play again until late July. He still managed to hit .310 with a .365 OBP in forty-six games, and Durocher, perhaps as a testament to how much he valued Irvin's leadership, named him to the 1952 All-Star team anyway.

In 1953, Irvin's individual accomplishments far outweighed the team's performance. Though they scored more runs than they allowed, 768 to 747, the team managed to post a 70-84 record. Still, Irvin managed to be an impact bat at age thirty-four, hitting .329 and posting an OBP of .406, with 21 home runs and 97 RBIs.

Age finally caught up to Irvin in 1954, but he was still an important cog in that year's championship season. He slumped to a very un-Irvin mark of .262 but still managed to get on base at a .363 clip, hit 19 home runs and compiled a .801 OPS. Not too shabby for a thirty-five-year-old with a bad ankle.

Of course, the Giants swept the heavily favored Cleveland Indians, who were coming off a record-setting 111-win season, and Irvin's legacy was punctuated by being part of Manhattan's last champions.

That year would mark his last full season with New York. He would spend half of the 1955 season in the minors and would enjoy his last full season in MLB with the Cubs in 1956. Irvin retired in 1957, just four games into the season.

While working on his book *The Soul of Baseball*, Joe Posnanski chronicled a conversation between legends Irvin and O'Neil.

> *"I was a different player by then," Irvin said. "I was still good. But I was not the same player."*
>
> *"I know," O'Neil said.*
>
> *Irvin continued: "I'm not complaining. I mean, I lived a good life. Better than most guys in the Negro Leagues. I got to play in the Major Leagues. I got to play in the World Series. I'm not complaining. It's just that people used to tell me how good I was, and I would tell them, 'You should have seen me when I could really play.'"*

After he retired, Irvin worked in public relations with Rheingold Brewery, as a scout with the New York Mets and as an assistant to the commissioner of baseball. In 1973, he was elected to the Baseball Hall of Fame by the Committee on Negro Baseball Leagues, becoming the fourth Negro Leaguer elected, following Satchel Paige, Josh Gibson and Buck Leonard.

To baseball authors like Staples, he was as an outstanding source for any book and, in Staples's case, a lifelong friend.

I had several chances to interview Monte Irvin over the years and could never make it happen. How I wished I had been able to do so.

4

WILLIE MAYS

I never saw a fucking ball go out of a fucking ballpark
so fucking fast in my fucking life.
—Leo Durocher

Hall of Fame manager Leo Durocher had a colorful way of putting things, and while some may object to the profanity, our epigraph certainly describes the greatness of Willie Mays.

If you don't believe Leo—who played with Babe Ruth—then you'll just have to believe Ron Healey.

My dad was a huge Brooklyn Dodgers fan growing up, and anyone who meets him—after doing a double take because he looks exactly like former Mets manager Terry Collins—soon realizes that he is a fountain of knowledge about the game he loves and the team that broke his heart.

I've learned many things from my father, and one of them is that greatness is not relegated to the team of the players you root for. His only blind spot is the Yankees, which he loathes and always will. But it's truly because of him that I can assess players in the objective way that I currently do.

As a kid in Flatbush, my dad loved Duke Snider. When he could save enough nickels to get a ticket to a game, he'd make a day out of it. He'd watch the "Dook" from the center-field bleachers during batting practice, shagging flies after he hit.

"Back then, during batting practice, they used old balls," remembered my dad. "Every now and then one of the players would ask for a new one,

Duke Snider was my dad's favorite player. *Photo by the Baseball Hall of Fame.*

and when Duke would catch it, he'd put it in his back pocket. We all knew what was going to happen. When BP was over, he would flip that new ball over his head, without looking, and one of us would be lucky enough to get a new ball to play with."

Now, stories like that would make you think that when I asked him who the best center fielder he ever saw was, he'd say the Duke. But he didn't. From the time I was a little boy, he always told the same story.

It was 1951, Mays has just been called up by the Giants. I had no idea who he was. My friend and I wound up going to Ebbets Field one day for a game against the Giants, which got rained out. We had our spiral notebooks to get autographs, so we waited in the rotunda for the players to come out. The players would exit through this one turnstile, so we waited there. You could always tell who the ballplayers were, they had short hair, had muscles and wore Ban-Lon shirts. ["Make sure you write Ban-Lon, so they know what I'm talking about," my dad told me.] *So this one guy comes out, looked like a ballplayer, and though we didn't recognize him, we asked him for his autograph. He said, "Sure kid." A few days later, I realized it was Willie Mays.*

"I loved the Duke, but Willie Mays is the best ballplayer I saw. He could do everything."

Now, if my dad's word isn't good enough for you (for shame!), how about Snider's teammate Carl Erskine?

"Several times, I have received questions in my fan mail asking me to choose the best player I ever saw. I have always said Mays because I saw him do so many things in so many ways to beat you, with his bat, his glove and his arm. He was the All-Star of All-Stars," Erskine told Smithsonian.com

I also asked a bunch of baseball fans who saw Mays, Mickey Mantle and Snider play.

"Saw all three often, Yankee fan since 1948, but Mays was clearly the best," said Howard Schwach, longtime editor of *The Wave* newspaper in Rockaway Beach. "Perhaps if Mickey had not stepped on that sprinkler [in the 1951 Series, on a ball hit by Willie], things might have been different, but he did."

Legendary broadcaster Spencer Ross, who has served as a play-by-play man for the Yankees, Knicks, Nets, Jets and Giants, shared this with me: "Mickey'd be the first to tell you Willie was the greatest of them all. He told it to me." Ross also added that while many argue for Joe DiMaggio (especially Yankees fans), "You can make the argument that he might have been as good as Willie in the field, but how could anyone be better defensively at that position than Willie Mays?"

"On two legs, Mickey Mantle would have been the greatest ballplayer who ever lived."—Nellie Fox (*Baseball Almanac*). *Photo by The Baseball Hall of Fame.*

Carlos Beltrán is the best Met to ever play center field. Despite an underwhelming first year at Shea Stadium, he hit .280 with 149 home runs, 208 doubles, 559 RBIs, 100 stolen bases and a .860 OPS in 3,640 plate appearances as a Met. When he retired, he joined Mays and Andre Dawson (as well as abusers of performance-enhancing drugs Alex Rodriguez and Barry Bonds) as the only players to have 500 doubles, 400 home runs and 300 stolen bases. Oddly, Beltrán's Cooperstown chances, which once seemed as a given (as his wearing a Mets cap when inducted), has now been thrown into limbo, given his involvement in the Houston Astros' sign-stealing scandal. The MLB investigation, which named Beltrán, also cost the former All-Star his first managing job, as the Mets and he decided to part ways just two months after he was hired to manage the club. Regardless, Beltrán, like the Duke, is a few steps behind the Mick and the Say Hey Kid.

My own memories of Mays come from other places: *Baseball's Youngest Big Leaguers* by John Devaney, the collection of Mets yearbooks my dad kept from 1962 (which he gave me to keep when I started writing this book), the MLB film of the 1973 World Series and the classic "Schaefer Circle" ad campaign. The latter was a stylistic series of commercials honoring the best of the best. Don't ask me why it always stuck in my brain when I think of Mays—I'm a Miller High Life guy myself. But it did. Maybe it was the intensity of the star in Mays's eyes or the muscles twitching in his forearms. As I said, I will always remember it.

The Devaney book made a lasting impression, maybe because I read it and re-read it so many times. It detailed Mays's now-legendary early years with his ballplaying father, William Howard Mays Sr., also known as Cat. It told the story of his childhood, with the younger Mays making believe he was Joe DiMaggio, and Willie's joining the Negro Leagues' Birmingham Black Barons at age seventeen.

I realized that Devaney's book was even better than I first thought after I read *Willie Mays: The Life, The Legend* by James S. Hirsch, which was published in 2010. Much like *Curb Your Enthusiasm* is the "real-life" version of *Seinfeld*, Hirsch's book was the adult version of Mays's life. Brilliantly written and well researched, the book painstakingly details Willie's early baseball life in Birmingham, where he met Lorenzo "Piper" Davis, the player-manager of the Barons.

The elder Mays always knew that the key to his son's talent was positive reinforcement. For Willie, who always played at the highest level, no insult or disparagement was going to make him play harder, but if he struggled, a helping hand and attitude was the way to get through to the teenager. Having played with Davis when both were younger, the elder Mays was able to ensure that Davis would understand how to handle Willie best. He also teamed up with Davis to begin Willie's education of the game.

Peppered with questions by both his dad and his manager, Willie soon learned that playing center field wasn't just about natural ability; it was about being the smartest guy on the field as well, a status that Mays quickly earned. Most outfielders of that era were taught to field ground balls on one knee, a conservative approach that limited the chance for a ball going behind them for extra bases. Davis saw that his pupil had a rocket for an arm and had the speed to make up for any misjudgment, so he directed Willie to be aggressive at all times. That advice changed everything, as described by Hirsch: "When Mays reached the major leagues, he stunned baserunners when he charged the ball—he played the outfield like the infield…using his oversized hand like a glove, he learned to charge and scoop up base hits with his right hand and throw the ball home in one fluid motion. 'Nobody,' Davis later said, 'and I mean nobody, ever saw anybody throw a ball from the outfield like him, or get rid of it so fast.'"

While becoming a fearless center fielder, Mays struggled when he first joined the Barons, especially at the plate, but he was a boy among men. Other kids his age were playing on their high school teams. To compensate, Davis constantly told his young charge "Watch and learn." Mays did and soaked up every bit of knowledge he could in the interim.

I hate to sound like a "get off my lawn" type of older guy, but while there are many players who embrace the analytics of the game, there are far too many today who do not work on—and teams that do not teach—the finer points of the game on the field. How many times have you watched a major league game and saw a player throw to the wrong base or try to advance on a ball hit in front of them or even fail to reach second base on a dropped fly ball because they put more emphasis on "stylin'" after a ball is hit?

Mays had style, sure, but much of it was based on beating the other team. The signature "basket catch," wrote James McMurry for Smithsonian.com, was "a confident and sophisticated move which was not being used in the game at that time and which also put him in a better position to throw the ball."

Despite Mays being one of the finest talents the Negro Leagues had to offer, the Yankees had no interest in his services. Despite firsthand evidence across town with Brooklyn—Jackie Robinson hit .342 in 1949, twenty-three-year-old Don Newcombe won a team-high 17 games and Roy Campanella hit 22 home runs—the Bronx passed. In his bio of former Yankee general manager George Weiss at the Society for American Baseball Research's website, SABR.org, my friend Dan Levitt noted that Weiss "presided over the greatest sustained run of excellence in baseball history," yet one imagines that, given the power and influence the Yankees had at that time, there would have been no World Series title lull between 1962 and 1977.

What were they thinking?

In 2009, John Klima, the author of *Willie's Boys: The 1948 Birmingham Black Barons, the Last Negro League World Series, and the Making of a Baseball Legend*, wrote that on May 29, 1949, Mays, eighteen, made his debut at the Polo Grounds. He played center field for the Barons, who were playing the New York Cubans, who rented the New York Giants' home field when they were out of town.

That was the first time Giants officials saw Mays. Their scouts were astonished at his advanced skills. That was also the first time Yankees scouts chose to ignore Mays. On the same trip, the Black Barons visited the Brooklyn

Bushwicks, a white semi-professional team whose general manager, Joe Press, was a part-time scout for the Yankees. Press booked Negro League teams like the Black Barons to play the Bushwicks and had a feel for the talent available. He liked Piper Davis, Birmingham's second baseman, but he loved center fielder Willie Mays. Press pleaded with Paul Krichell, the Yankees' head scout, to see Mays. In a letter to Krichell, Press raved about players but expressed dismay that the Yankees had chosen to ignore black prospects. "You could have had practically all of them, just for the asking," Press wrote, naming several players, including Davis and Mays. When the Black Barons returned to play the Cubans at the Polo Grounds on June 11, 1950, the Yankees sent a scout, Bill McCorry, but again decided to not pursue Mays, who signed with the Giants nine days later.

As insufferable as some Yankees fans can be, imagine if Mays and Ernie Banks had joined Mantle. Yes, you read that right: Ernie Banks easily could have been a Yankee.

Klima expounds on the Banks question:

When the Yankees did explore the Negro leagues market, they did so with the help of Tom Baird, a white man who owned the Kansas City Monarchs and was a registered member of the Kansas Ku Klux Klan.…In a letter dated June 20, the day Mays signed with the Giants, [Baird wrote] "I signed Ernest Banks, 19-year-old shortstop, and he looks like he will make a hell of a good ballplayer."…The Yankees never wrote back about Banks.

Instead, the Giants and the aforementioned Durocher would be the beneficiary.

Mays would dominate the minors in his short tenure, hitting .353 in Trenton in 1950. He also was the beneficiary of even more tutelage in the nuances of the game. His manager in Trenton, Frank "Chick" Genovese, and the GM, Bill McKechnie Jr. (namesake son of the Hall of Fame manager), spent hours peppering Mays with questions, mostly about pitching. When Mays asked why they were asking him pitching questions, McKechnie replied, "The only way to be a smart hitter is to start thinking like a pitcher." It must have worked, because the next season, this time in Triple-A Minneapolis, he was hitting .477 after thirty-five games when Durocher's pestering—he had asked for Mays to be on the 1951 Opening Day roster—finally paid off. Durocher would immediately— and thereafter—serve as a surrogate father for Mays. But the presence of Monte Irvin would be especially helpful, especially at the beginning of Willie's career.

"He taught me a lot of things about life," Mays told NPR's Laura Wagner in 2016 after Irvin passed. "I already knew how to play the game, but sometimes you need a little more. You need to know how to treat people. You need to know how when you hit a home run, you run around the bases—you don't stop and show anybody up. Thinking was more important to him than just playing the game."

Mays, who'd always responded to positive reinforcement, once again had two mentors helping him adjust to life in the biggest city in the big leagues.

"Although Willie had a little trouble adjusting to major-league pitching at first, he caught everything in sight and could throw runners out from about anywhere in the outfield," said Irvin. "In fact, when Willie joined us Durocher took the other outfielders, Don Mueller and me, aside and told us to let Willie have any ball he could get to since he had tremendous range and such a rifle arm. It got to the point that it was a treat to come to the ballpark each day to see what great catch or throw Willie would make."

Willie showed flashes that year offensively—his first major-league hit was a home run off Braves left-hander and eventual Hall of Famer Warren Spahn—but it was his amazing plays in the vast expanse of the Polo Grounds that likely made him Rookie of the Year.

Mays would play just thirty-four games in 1952 before being drafted into the U.S. Army, and the assignment must have been weighing on his mind, because he hit just .236. In an illustration of the kind of impact he had in just one season, the Brooklyn crowd at Ebbets Field—where cheering a Giant was *infamnia*—gave Willie a standing ovation. Making the moment even more surreal, legendary organist Gladys Gooding played "I'll See You in My Dreams."

When Mays returned in 1954, it was more of a nightmare for Dodger fans.

Durocher told everyone within earshot that Mays would hit .300 and hit 30 homers in 1954, which was quite optimistic, as SABR's John Saccoman noted: "[Mays's] major-league resume up to that time, in 155 games,

Willie Mays, the perfect ballplayer. *Photo by The Baseball Hall of Fame.*

included a .266 batting average, .459 slugging percentage, and 24 home runs—an impressive start to a career, but nothing to make one think he could take a mediocre team past the Dodgers, a group that included Jackie Robinson, Duke Snider, and Roy Campanella."

But he did, and his remarkable 1954 season—.345/.411/.667 with 41 HRs and 110 RBIs—would not only win him an MVP but also propel the Giants to a World Series title. It was the last Fall Classic the New York baseball Giants would ever play in, and the sweep of the highly favored Cleveland Indians was punctuated by what may be the greatest play ever made in a World Series game.

It didn't just help win a game; it may also have won the Series. The Indians (111-43) were so good in 1954 that the Yankees won 103 games and finished 8 games back of the Tribe. Led by ace pitchers Bob Lemon and Early Wynn, Cleveland led the American League with a stellar 2.78 earned-run average (the league average was 3.72). The offense had Larry Doby (32 HRs, 126 RBI) and Al Rosen (.300, 24 HRs, 102 RBIs). Few picked the New Yorkers, figuring if the Indians could outlast the Yankees, they could make quick work of the crosstown G-Men.

Yet, it was all over after Game One, a game that was up for grabs in the top of the eighth. The score was 2–2, Doby was on second, Rosen was on first and Vic Wertz was at the plate.

Before we get back to the game, a quick word on Wertz. He is known best—let's be honest, only—for his role in this 1954 play we are about to describe. A quick look at his stats for that season shows that he hit .257/.330/.422 with 15 homers and 61 RBIs in 123 games. But Wertz was more than that. After you read this chapter, check out Mark Armour's bio piece on him at SABR.org. It's really interesting. One takeaway I'll share here: "Were it not for Mays's sensational play, Wertz would have registered the first five-hit game in World Series history, a feat later accomplished only by Paul Molitor, in 1982."

Back to the game. Wertz crushed the pitch to deep center, and given the vast expanse of the Polo Grounds (the center-field fence was 455 feet away), it would be a tall task to keep a run from scoring.

Mays described the play to the *Sporting News*' Roger Kahn:

> *Wertz hits it. A solid sound. I learned a lot from the sound of the ball on the bat. Always did. I could tell from the sound whether to come in or go back. This time I'm going back, a long way back, but there is no doubt in my mind. I am going to catch this ball....But that wasn't the problem. The*

problem was Larry Doby on second base. On a deep fly to center field at the Polo Grounds, a runner could score all the way from second. I've done that myself and more than once. So if I make the catch, which I will, and Larry scores from second, they still get the run that puts them ahead. All the time I'm running back, I'm thinking, "Willie, you've got to get this ball back into the infield."

Mays "travel[ed] on the wings of wind," wrote the New York Times' *John Drebinger, "to make one of his most amazing catchers." Mays, the NL Most Valuable Player in his first full season, spending most of the previous two in the armed forces, whirled around and heaved the ball to the infield as Doby tagged and raced to third. "Durocher was standing in front of me in the dugout," former Giants batboy Bobby Weinstein told the author. "He turned around and said 'Oh no.' And then he saw Mays run the ball down." After the game, Mays took his fielding exploit in stride, "I had it all the way," he said. "There was nothing too hard about it."*

The throw, according to Mays, was what he was worried about. "I have to turn very hard and short and throw the ball from exactly the point I caught it," he told Kahn. "The momentum goes into my turn and up through my legs and into my throw."

"Consider this," wrote ESPN's Jeff Merron. "Mays' throw only allowed Doby to advance from second to third and held—held!—Al Rosen on first."

Merrons also described the reaction to the play in his essay, "The True 'Catch' Story."

A few weeks after the series ended, Pittsburgh GM Joe E. Brown told the *Sporting News*:

> *The catch itself was tremendous, but to me that wasn't the big thing and it's strange that not much attention has been given to it. It's what Willie did after catching the ball. He started to fall but as he did, he spun around and got rid of the ball. He made a strong throw off balance and while falling. Do you realize that if he had fallen down holding onto the ball, that runner might have scored all the way from second? That could have won the game for Cleveland and could have changed the whole Series.*

The game was eventually won by Dusty Rhodes's pinch-hit, three-run homer in the tenth, which barely cleared the right-field fence, just 257 feet away from home plate. The pop fly was described as a "Chinese Home Run," the politically incorrect verbiage of the day describing a "cheap" home run.

"We were beaten by the longest out and the shortest home run of the year," Al Lopez, skipper of the Indians, told the Associated Press. After the Series, he told the *Sporting News*, "Losing the first game hurt us the most.... Willie Mays made that great catch on Wertz' drive and we were never the same."

It was Mays's signature moment of his career, and it happened in New York. But, really, the name of the play should be "The Throw."

Willie had an even better season in 1955, and really, he should have been the MVP. He led the NL in home runs (51), slugging (.659) and OPS (1.059, a career-high) while finishing second in batting average, runs and RBIs. Yet he finished fourth in the voting behind Brooklyn's Roy Campanella. While the "Boys of Summer" were winning their first—and last—Series across town, the Giants followed up their historic season with a third-place finish, 80-74, which cost Durocher his job. His replacement, Bill Rigney, was so intent on creating his own identity that he soon alienated Mays, who did not care for being publicly criticized. Though he still put up All-Star numbers, something was missing with Willie in 1956; he hit .296 with 36 home runs and 84 RBIs, despite hitting a 1.006 OPS with RISP. He did lead the league with 40 stolen bases, but with the exception of a young Bill White at first base (22 HRs) and All-Star Johnny Antonelli (20-13, 2.86 ERA) on the mound, the Giants were terrible (67-87), finishing sixth, twenty-six games out.

In Hirsch's book, he wrote that in 1957, Rigney reconciled with his star and Mays had a great season. Rigney came to realize that Mays needed a father figure, a role favored by Durocher. Rigney said, "If I had to do it over again, I think I might have been a little more active in his life." The numbers seem to bear that out. In Mays's last season in New York, he had an OPS of 1.033, hitting 35 home runs with 97 RBIs and a .333 batting average, a .407 OBP, scoring 112 runs and stealing 38 bases. However, the Giants struggled all year, drawing just 653,923 fans to the Polo Grounds, an average of 8,493 a game, both marks being the worst in the NL.

Willie's time as a New York Giant was now, and one would think that he would have been welcomed with open arms in San Francisco. Sadly, for much of Willie's time there, despite some wonderful seasons, the Bay Area fans preferred Willie McCovey and Orlando Cepeda, whom they considered their own.

Red Smith wrote in the *New York Times*:

> In 1958...the welcome accorded Willie Mays was restrained, if not downright cool. Willie played center field, a social error in San Francisco.

As far as the residents of the Bay Area were concerned, that position was the exclusive property of the homegrown demigod, Joseph Paul DiMaggio, and anybody who tried to muscle in was an imposter. Though Willie led the Giants with a batting average of .347 and 29 home runs, the fans voted Cepeda the team's most valuable player. Not long afterward, Nikita Khrushchev visited California and as his car moved through the San Francisco streets, crowds along the curb applauded. "What kind of town is this?" demanded the late Frank Coniff, an old Giant fan who was covering the tour for the Hearst papers. "They cheer Khrushchev and boo Willie Mays!"

Hirsch explained that much of the resentment came from the San Francisco media, which found Mays a difficult interviewee and aloof—except when the New York writers were in town. Writers like the aforementioned Kahn, Milton Gross, Jimmy Cannon and others were familiar to him, and they conversed like old friends. Which they were, according to Mays. "I want to know a writer before I answer his questions. I don't want to be put on the spot," he told the *New York Times*.

According to Hirsch, Mays also agreed to cooperate with the *Call-Bulletin* newspaper on a ghost-written column, infuriating the writers from the three other Bay Area dailies.

"The general press box appraisal of Mays is that he is an All-American knothead," wrote the *San Francisco News'* Bud Spencer. "Willie's problem is that he needs to be driven. Anybody got a whip?"

That kind of racist idiocy is more than enough reason to ignore Mays's time in San Francisco, for this book at least.

Mets owner Joan Payson never stopped trying to get Mays back to New York and had offered very large sums to the Giants over the years to make it happen. In 1962, when she bought the Mets, she had to divest herself of her share of the Giants. According to Vince Guerrieri, in an article on OZY.com titled "The Heiress Who Loved Baseball So Much, She Bought Her Own Team," the shares were worth an estimated $680,000 then, so she proposed a trade: Instead of the cash, she'd take her favorite player, Willie Mays.

Stoneham said no, but he didn't a decade later. On Mother's Day in 1972, Willie Mays returned to New York. He'd have the old familiar "NY" on his cap, but, while memorable, his return to Gotham would be complicated.

Mays wasn't overly happy with being traded without being consulted by a man he thought to be family, but Charles Stoneham's team was in financial disarray, and by trading him to the Mets and Payson, he knew that Mays would be taken care of after his eventual retirement.

Publicly, Mays told the *New York Times*, "When you come back to New York, it's like coming back to paradise."

Mays may have been glad to come back to New York, and the Mets needed his leadership as much as he needed their money. "Besides assuming his current salary, the Mets agreed to keep him for at least three years as a coach at $75,000 a year after he quits playing—which presumably could be at the end of this season or next," wrote the *Times*' Joe Durso after the deal was official.

The Mets' manager was Yogi Berra, who once famously said that "Ninety percent of the game is half mental." He could have been talking about Mays, because there were few players on the field smarter than the kid from Alabama. However, when Mays came to the Mets, the team was still shell-shocked, as the beloved Gil Hodges had died of a heart attack just a few months earlier in spring training. When the press met Willie for the first time after the deal was announced, Willie said, "I'm looking forward to playing and helping, but not embarrassing myself." He was hitting .185 at the time of the trade and had been feuding with Giants manager Charlie Fox after he was benched without being consulted.

"He can still spell Tommie Agee in center field sometimes," Berra said, "and he can play first base for us against left-handed pitching." Unfortunately, because of injuries—and probably because of M. Donald Grant, who said: "This deal can help us at the gate."—Berra was forced to play Mays far more than he or Mays had imagined. He was also batting first and third far more than a player of his advanced age should have been. He still managed to hit .267 with an astounding .402 OBP, and his leadership was welcomed.

It was a tumultuous season: Hodges's death; a trade for Rusty Staub (who was supposed to be the team's impact bat, only to be lost for most of the year after getting hit by a pitch); as well as the infamous deal with the Angels that sent Nolan Ryan packing for Jim Fregosi.

It was also the season in which left-hander Jon Matlack was named the National League's Rookie of the Year (15-10, 2.32 ERA). "I count myself as one of the lucky people who got to play with Willie," Matlack told Paul Post from *Sports Collectors Digest*. "He was like a dad at times. A group of us might be out having a bite after a game, with a day game the next day. He'd look at me and say, 'Kid, you're pitching tomorrow. You'd better get home and go to sleep!' Just stuff like that. It was a neat relationship."

Tom Seaver, who was the team's unquestioned leader, was a huge Mays fan growing up in Fresno. The first time Mays was slated to start in center when Seaver pitched, he approached the pitcher to discuss the way he would pitch to the opposing batters, and where Mays should position himself. "Part of me thinks, isn't this ironic, but the professional part of me thinks, isn't this spectacular," Seaver told Hirsch. "So I went down the lineup, and then I said, 'If I want to move you, I'll turn around and move my glove that way, and you move until I lose eye contact, and that's it." And then he said, 'We'll adjust the last six outs.' Then I said, 'Absolutely.'"

Seaver concluded by saying that in his twenty years in professional baseball, Mays was the only position player to ever ask him how he was going to pitch to an opposing player.

Mays's last season was by far the worst of his career. Again, injuries to key Mets during the course of the season made Berra use Mays far more than he wanted to, but no one was more frustrated than Willie. Physically, he looked as good as he did when he was roaming the Polo Grounds, but his knees were betraying him, and his once-powerful throwing arm was no more. But even at forty-two, he was still clutch, owning a .817 OPS with runners in scoring position.

George Stone, who was a key contributor to the Mets' unlikely 1973 NL pennant, was another player who valued Mays as a teammate. "Willie was valuable in the clubhouse. He always had something going on; a real loosey-goosey guy," recalled Stone for the *Utica Observer-Dispatch*'s Don Laible.

During the NLCS with the Cincinnati Reds, Mets shortstop Bud Harrelson and Pete Rose got into the now-infamous scuffle. According to Stone, after the game, Mays sought out Harrelson to discuss what took place. "Bud and Willie went into the trainer's room. Willie counseled him on what to say to the media. That's where he [Mays] was so valuable to the ball club. Willie had done everything, seen everything, and knew what to say."

The image of Mays dropping two fly balls in Oakland in Game 2 of the World Series was pretty terrible, but the final hit of Mays's career was a twelfth-inning RBI single up the middle to put the Mets ahead in a game they hung on to win.

The Mets would lose the Series after holding a 3-2 lead going into Game 6, and whose fault it was doesn't really matter, but Mays went out of baseball the same way he came in, as a World Series player.

His time as a Mets coach was troubled, mostly because Grant thought he was a piece of property to be dictated to, not an asset to help the club be the best it could be. It ended when Commissioner Bowie Kuhn thought that Mays and Mantle working for Bally's in Atlantic City was bad for baseball.

The Mets have tried over the years to re-engage with Mays, but this current regime is almost as bad at dealing with former players as Grant was. However, there is a little-told, albeit wonderful gem about Mays and recently retired David Wright.

According to the *New York Times'* David Waldstein, Wright and Mays developed a friendship dating to the final day at Shea Stadium, September 28, 2008. After the game, a demoralizing 4–2 loss to the Marlins that cost the Mets the postseason for the second year in a row, the Hall of Famer found a way to sit with Wright in the Mets' clubhouse.

For about half an hour, they talked baseball. "It wasn't a great day because of the circumstances," said Wright. "But really, what I take away from that day, beyond the game, was the chance to meet Mays."

The two reunited again in 2010 at AT&T Field, in a room off the Giants' clubhouse before an afternoon game. "That was one of the coolest things. We shut the door and talked baseball. You talk to coaches or people who have been around the game for a long time about the best players of all time, his name is always one of the first, if not the first, to be mentioned," Wright said. "When a guy like that wants to talk to you and call you over to talk about the game and talk shop, it means a lot."

Award-winning journalist Pete Hamill—who wrote a glowing review of Hirsch's book for the *New York Times* when it came out—eloquently captured the essence of Mays, which is a perfect way to end this chapter:

> *The young should know that there was once a time when Willie Mays lived among the people who came to the ballpark. That on Harlem summer days he would join the kids playing stickball on St. Nicholas Place in Sugar Hill and hold a broom-handle bat in his large hands, wait for the pink rubber spaldeen to be pitched, and routinely hit it four sewers. The book explains what that sentence means.*
>
> *Above all, the story of Willie Mays reminds us of a time when the only performance-enhancing drug was joy.*

5

BABE RUTH

Heroes get remembered, but legends never die.
—*Babe Ruth*

Hollywood has never had much luck making a movie about Babe Ruth, so while his legend may never die, it's been tarnished a bit.

For starters, the John Goodman vehicle *The Babe* is horrendous.

There's no excuse for a film that was made in 1992 to be so poorly crafted. Goodman is a fine actor. To *Rolling Stone*'s Peter Travers, Goodman was "ideally cast as George Herman Ruth, the incorrigible fat kid who rose to glory as the Babe." But that's what happens when you ask a music journalist to review a sports film.

Maybe it's because Hollywood never asked a baseball fan to cast Ruth, whose legend portrays a bigger-than-life character with gargantuan appetites. Perhaps that demands a casting director to try to find an actor cut from the same cloth. And Goodman fits that bill.

However, Ruth wasn't fat as a child, as the movie portrays. Nor was he a porculent with the Red Sox or during his early career with the Yankees, a choice seemingly made by the director, actor and whoever else was involved with that monstrosity of a film.

Just ask Hall of Fame pitcher Waite Hoyt, who spent ten years with the Yankees as Ruth's teammate. He cleared up that subject in an interview for the National Baseball Hall of Fame in 1981. "To begin with, let me tell you this about Babe Ruth. He was not fat," said Hoyt. "And he did not have skinny legs. He had rather tapered ankles, that's true. But…the calves of his legs were very good sized, and he was not fat. He had a big chest and he had a very small fanny and he was not big around the waist."

The Babe Ruth Story, starring William Bendix, is just as horrible, and I agree with A. Morris, a reviewer on Turner Classic Movies' website, who wrote, "If some movies of a genre are so bad they could represent illness…then this is the French disease of sports films."

Bendix—another fine actor—was completely miscast as Ruth, and the movie is mind-numbingly bad.

In NBC's 1991 film *Babe Ruth*, adapted from Robert Creamer's biography *Babe: The Legend Comes to Life*, there are some attempts at accuracy. Tony Award–winning actor Stephen Lang played the Big Bam, and like every great actor, he did his homework. Lang did his best to show how Ruth eventually became heavier as he got older.

It's a TV movie, so it was limited in its scope and a little hard to watch, but Lang made a credible effort to capture baseball's greatest player. Unfortunately, it's mostly wasted, because Lang used a prosthetic nose—Goodman did as well—to resemble Ruth. In that, we never truly believe that we're watching Babe Ruth. Instead, we are watching a good actor wearing a clown nose.

Barry Levinson is the only director who's ever come close to capturing the Babe. In *The Natural* (my favorite baseball movie of all time), veteran actor Joe Don Baker plays "The Whammer," who is clearly based on Ruth.

In case there was any doubt, sportswriter Max Mercy (played with relish by Robert Duvall) describes Whammer as "best there ever was. Best there is now and the best there ever will be."

Levinson, a baseball fan and an Academy Award winner who has directed some of my favorite films, had considered former major leaguers Boog Powell and Harmon Killebrew for the role of Whammer. I tried contacting Levinson to ask him why he chose Baker, but to no avail.

Baker's Whammer hits all the right notes, with the lone exception of his overt rudeness. Ruth certainly could be crude and was terrible with names, calling everyone under a certain age "kid" and older men "doc." Women, on the other hand, were "sweety," "baby" or "honey." But Whammer is seen in *The Natural* as a bad guy.

Ruth played himself in *Pride of the Yankees* and was praised by *Time* magazine for his "fidelity and considerable humor." What they didn't mention is that he was hospitalized after he lost fifty pounds for the film and nearly died in the process.

Maybe the moral of the story is that the only person who could play Ruth was Ruth himself.

"Why start the chapter about Ruth like this?," you might be asking yourself. I think the point is that Ruth is hard to cast because he is so hard to define. Also, with so much written about the Babe over the years, it seems almost redundant to talk about why he's the greatest player ever. But as time marches on, Ruth's standing as the best baseball player of all time has come under some scrutiny.

The late, great sportswriter Maury Allen once wrote that Babe Ruth

> *never played a night game, he never hit against fireball relief pitching, he never traveled cross-country for a night game and played a day game the next day, he never performed before millions of television viewers, he never had to run on artificial turf. It is the changes in the game, the modern factors that have made the game more difficult, that bring Babe in here as number three, behind [Willie] Mays and [Hank] Aaron. His feats were heroic. So were theirs. They simply did them under tougher conditions.*

Now, with all due respect to Maury, I'm not going to try to tell you that Aaron and Mays don't deserve to be in the same sentence as Ruth—they do—but Ruth was simply better.

The Angels' two-way sensation Shohei Ohtani is supposed to be the next Babe, a great starting pitcher who can also bat cleanup. Hopes were high that the former Nippon Ham Fighter could become the first player since Ruth in 1918 and 1919 to amass both 200 plate appearances and 100 innings pitched in the same season.

In 2018, Ohtani won his second straight start to begin his rookie season, and the twenty-three-year-old had also hit a home run in each of his previous three games as a designated hitter for Los Angeles, something Ruth never accomplished, as the *Washington Post*'s Des Bieler was excited to point out. He quoted Angel catcher Martin Maldonado gushing about his teammate:

> *"He looks like a hitter when he's batting and looks like a pitcher when he's pitching. It's impressive. We haven't seen that before."*
>
> *Well, we haven't seen it in about a century, anyway, but even Ruth didn't match some of Ohtani's two-way accomplishments. Sure, it's early in the season, making the Angels' phenom something like the Sultan of Small Sample Sizes, but it's safe to say he's off to a historic, uniquely impressive start.*

Hollywood has never been kind to Babe Ruth. Maybe it never will be. *Photo by The Baseball Hall of Fame.*

Well, the twenty-three-year-old did perform well at the plate, compiling a 152 Weighted Runs Created Plus (wRC+) (which, according to FanGraphs, "quantifies the most important part of a batter's job—creating runs—and normalizes it, so we can compare players who play in different ballparks and even different eras"). It was good enough for ninth in the majors.

But he managed just 51 innings before blowing out his elbow, and he didn't pitch in 2019. He's twenty-three, so he has a bright future. I want the kid to be great. It's not his fault that he's surrounded by idiots who insist on making unrealistic comparisons.

Look, by the time Ruth was twenty-three, in 1918, he had produced a 189 wRC+ (thanks Fangraphs), was a two-time 20-game winner, had won three World Series with the Red Sox and had pitched over 1,000 innings (including back-to-back 300-plus innings pitched in 1916–17). He also set a Fall Classic record for scoreless innings along the way. (It would last until another Gotham Baseball legend, Whitey Ford, broke it in 1961.)

And then he came to New York. Game over, everybody else.

As Leigh Montville wrote in *The Big Bam*: "The marriage between the Babe and New York City had every chance to be perfect; he was built for the New York of 1920 and the New York of 1920 was built for him. He was the muscle man coming to a muscle city in a muscle time."

Prior to 1920, the Yankees had not been a muscle team. Since joining the American League in 1903, the then-Highlanders won ninety-two games in 1904 (thanks to Jack Chesbro's forty-one wins) but blew the pennant on the last day of the season. In 1906, Chesbro and "Prince" Hal Chase helped the Highlanders win ninety games but finished second to the eventual World Champion White Sox.

Ruth (twenty-five) celebrated his first season in Gotham by destroying the baseball, hitting 54 home runs in 457 at-bats, more home runs than any other major-league team besides the Phillies. He led all of baseball in runs (158), RBIs (135), walks (150), OBP (.532), slugging (.847), OPS (1.379) and OPS+ (255).

The Yankees, who had been sharing the Polo Grounds with the New York Giants since 1913, had always been welcome tenants in Manhattan. That changed in 1920.

The Yankees improved their 1919 record (80-59 in a war-shortened season) to 95-59 with Ruth but missed the pennant by three games. However, they outdrew their landlords, with an MLB-best 1,289,422 to Giant manager John McGraw's team's 929,609, prompting the Giants to issue an eviction notice.

Cooler heads prevailed in the offseason. Despite McGraw reportedly saying that the Yankees should "move to some out-of-the-way place, like Queens," the Giants clearly liked the money Ruth was bringing in. The Yankees would outdraw the Giants for the next two seasons, so McGraw—who hated Ruth—took solace in his team's World Series wins over the Yankees in 1921 and 1922.

Privately, McGraw loathed Ruth for another reason: sour grapes.

According to the Baseball Hall of Fame's Dylan Drolette, in 1914, McGraw tried to acquire the contract of a kid he had seen pitch against the

Newark Indians of the International League. McGraw contacted the owner of the IL's Baltimore Orioles, offering $5,000 for the lefty's services. But the Orioles's owner, Jack Dunn—who once played for former Oriole McGraw in New York—said no. McGraw was furious.

In 1921, Ruth hit 104 home runs. Well, that's what baseball historian and Ruth expert Bill Jenkinson states in his excellent book *The Year Babe Ruth Hit 104 Home Runs*. I have interviewed Jenkinson on a number of occasions. As earnest as he is in discussing the greatness of Ruth, his research—using spray charts and graphics to prove his case—is convincing.

"That season, Babe hit a combination of at least 40 triples, doubles and fly ball outs in various American League parks that easily would have soared over modern-day fences," Jenkinson wrote.

Jenkinson also unearths other drives called foul that would have been home runs under the current fair/foul rule implemented in 1931. He estimates that Ruth lost at least 50 home runs that way. Before 1931, umpires called balls fair or foul based on where they landed in the stands, as opposed to where they left the field of play. Since many stadiums weren't equipped with foul poles during Ruth's day—and those that did were much shorter—it was tough for umpires to properly judge the flight of the ball.

That would give Ruth 764 career home runs, more than Hank Aaron (755) and Barry Bonds (762). Given the new equation, Ruth also hit his 764 home runs in 3,915 fewer at-bats than Aaron and 1,398 fewer than Bonds.

But I digress.

In any event, in 1921, while Ruth broke his own home-run record with 59, the rest of the league had started to catch up. Well, sorta. The Yankees led the MLB in home runs in 1921 with 134; no other team even got to 90, and the league average that year was 59 home runs per team, the same number Ruth hit all by himself.

More important, Ruth's 1921 season helped the Yankees win their first pennant, thanks to a late September series at defending champs Cleveland in which they took three of four, breaking away to clinch the AL flag a few days later.

Ruth finished the regular season with 59 home runs, batting .378—third behind Harry Hellman (.394) and Ty Cobb (.389)—while slugging an MLB-best .846.

In the Series against the Giants, all of it played in the Polo Grounds, the Yankees blew a 2-0 Series lead after Ruth badly scraped his elbow during Game 2. The doctors told him not to play; he played anyway, and the Yankees lost, five games to three. Ruth did hit .316 and hit his first World

Series home runs, but the Giants pitching staff was in control for most of the Fall Classic.

Losing the Series was bad enough. Many aspects of what happened afterward is an underreported aspect of Ruth's life that many ignore, I guess in part because it doesn't fit their narrative of Ruth's records not meaning as much because he only played against white ballplayers.

History tells us that after the 1921 Series, Ruth chose to defy the commissioner of baseball, Judge Kenesaw Mountain Landis, by going through with a post-Series barnstorming tour. There was a rule on the books that prohibited World Series participants from playing in exhibition games during the offseason. The explanation given is that it would lessen the importance of the Series as the crown jewel of the season. The players didn't really pay too much attention to it, as barnstorming could put money in their pockets they'd otherwise have to earn working a real job. So, despite the rule, Ruth asked Yankee GM Ed Barrow if he could go through with the barnstorming tour. Barrow said yes, but only if Ruth asked Landis first.

Ruth, never a fan of authority, procrastinated and didn't call Landis until a day before the tour was supposed to begin. Landis, not amused, responded by asking Ruth to meet with him to discuss the issue. Ruth declined, saying he had to travel to the first game in Buffalo the next day. Landis exploded, denied Ruth permission and hung up on him.

According to Landis biographer David Pietrusza (*Judge and Jury: The Life and Times of Judge Kenesaw Mountain Landis*), the judge remarked: "Who the hell does that big ape think he is? That blankety-blank! If he goes on that trip it will be one of the sorriest things he has ever done."

You see, Ruth had broken this rule before. American League president Ban Johnson had issued a similar "no barnstorming" decree after the 1916 Series, but Ruth and many of his Red Sox teammates briefly toured New England anyway. The result: the players were fined $100 each. In fact, the rule had been indifferently enforced over the years, but interestingly, Landis seemed to especially care about the rule after the '21 Series.

Could the harsher response be due to the fact that the Babe Ruth All-Stars barnstorming schedule included games against Negro League teams, including the famed Kansas City Monarchs?

Maybe Landis was threatened by the idea of the game's most popular figure playing with black ballplayers. Ruth had played against black ballplayers before and, unlike many of his contemporaries, had no problem with it. He seemed to enjoy the competition. In turn, the teams and their fans flocked to Ruth.

"It sent a tremendous signal…an enormously powerful message," said Jenkinson. Besides playing, Jenkinson said, Ruth would sit with black players in the dugouts, talk and socialize with them before and after games and mingle in the segregated stands. He scheduled games in locations where interracial competition was not only against local norms but also against the law.

Ruth never seemed to mind sharing a baseball field with black players, and despite being the target of racial slurs since his youth—there were those who believed Ruth was of mixed race—he played against Negro League All-Star teams in rural Kansas and Oklahoma, territory under the influence of the Ku Klux Klan.

According to Jenkinson, Ruth's willingness to embrace mixed-race baseball was the real threat to Landis. Ruth would soon learn that the commissioner was no Ban Johnson.

> *Confident that any punishment would be comparable to his 1916 reprimand, Ruth embarked on his tour. However, after just five games, Yankees co-owner Tillinghast L'Hommedieu Huston intercepted Ruth in Scranton, Pennsylvania, and convinced him that the Judge meant business. Babe canceled the remainder of the schedule and awaited his fate. When Landis suspended Ruth for the first five weeks of the 1922 season, the country was shocked. Even President Warren G. Harding voiced his support for the Babe.*

The ensuing drama resulted in the barnstorming rule being removed by July 1922, but Ruth was forced to serve out his suspension, which he did until May 20. To appease Ruth during his exile, manager Miller Huggins named Ruth the Yankees' new on-field captain prior to the season. It wouldn't last long. Just five days after his return to on-field play, the Babe was tossed from a game for throwing dust in umpire George Hildebrand's face. Ruth then climbed into the stands to confront a heckler. Ban Johnson ordered Ruth stripped of his captaincy. The controversy didn't stop Ruth from his annual bludgeoning of AL pitching or the Yankees from winning another pennant, but the 1922 AL pennant chase was one that had a significant impact.

I don't have space here to chronicle that remarkable race, but I urge you to check out "The 1922 Browns-Yankees Pennant Race" by Paul W. Greenwell, which you can find at the Society for American Baseball Research. It's a great read.

Ruth would appear in only 110 games, but he'd still bat .315, smash 35 home runs and drive in 99 runs. He also led the league in slugging (.672) and

OPS (1.106). With the Yankees slated to open their palatial new stadium in 1923, this would be the last chance for Ruth to prove to McGraw once and for all that he and the Yanks were the top cats in town.

It did not happen, as, in the '22 World Series, McGraw's pitching staff threw Ruth a steady diet of slow breaking balls to which he never adjusted. Ruth's 2 hits in 17 at-bats was no glaring stat. Giant pitchers held the Yankees to just a .203 average and a .250 OBP for the entire Series, by virtue of a 0.870 ERA by five starters. It was technically a 4–0 sweep, albeit with one tie game. (Game 2 was a 3–3 stalemate called due to darkness after ten innings.)

Perhaps the loudest critic was the *New York Sun*'s Joe Vila, who wrote: "The exploded phenomenon didn't surprise the smart fans who long ago realized he couldn't hit brainy pitching. Ruth therefore is no longer a wonder. The baseball public is onto his real worth as a batsman, and in the future, let us hope he will attract just ordinary attention."

If Vila was around today, his comment would have been known as a "hot take" that would have "broken Twitter." Translation: Ruth fans would have lost their minds, and New York Giants fans would have returned the favor.

The 1922 season and World Series would prove to be the first real crossroads for Ruth. His suspension drew criticism from most New York newspapers; his on-field conduct was terrible; and he constantly fought with umpires, his own manager and even his teammates. His off-the-field behavior, never chronicled by the sportswriters of the day but witnessed by those same sportswriters, who would play cards with the Babe, was quite reprehensible.

At a special banquet held for Ruth in November 1922 at the Elks Club in Manhattan, state senator (soon to be New York City mayor) James J. Walker stood up and called Ruth out, as Leigh Montville captured in his book *The Big Bam*:

> "*Babe Ruth is not only a great athlete he's also a great fool…," said Walker, as the crowd gasped in disbelief. "You are making a bigger salary than anyone ever received as a ball player, but the bigger the salary the bigger the fool you have become.…Worst of all, first of all, you have let down the kids of America…everywhere in America, on every vacant lot where kids play baseball…hospitals too, where crippled children dream of movement…they think of you their hero. They look up to you, worship you, and then what happens? You carouse and abuse your great body. It is exactly as if Santa Claus himself suddenly were to take off his beard to reveal the features of a villain. The kids have seen their idol shattered and their dreams broken.*"

There has always been speculation that this was staged by Ruth's agent and public-relations mastermind, Christy Walsh. Reports of Ruth sobbing were inconsistent, and Walker was a notoriously corrupt politician. But for at least one season, it worked.

In 1923, Yankee Stadium—"The House That Ruth Built"—became the Bambino's playground, and his teammates joined in, pummeling every AL team that came to town. They won more home games (46) than any other team in the league—as well as more on the road (52)—and finished 16 games in front of player-manager Ty Cobb's Detroit Tigers. (That must have been a fun clubhouse that season.)

Ruth's 1923 was ridiculous. He hit .393 (it didn't lead the AL, as the Tigers' Harry Heilmann hit .403) and led the team in almost every other category: runs (151), home runs (41), RBIs (130), walks (170), OBP (.545), slugging (.764) and OPS (1.309).

Maybe he heard McGraw's snickering in his head. Or maybe it was Vila's criticisms, or being called a fool in a room full of New York City swells. But Ruth left nothing to chance in the 1923 Series against the Giants. The World Series MVP Award didn't exist then, but if it had, the wonderful Yankees blog *Pinstripe Alley* says it clearly would have been Ruth, who hit .368 in the six games, with 3 home runs and a 1.556 OPS.

Ruth's greatness would never be questioned again.

Except that it would.

In 1924, as Appel puts it in his masterwork *Pinstripe Empire*, the Yankees managed a strong season. It was just the Washington Senators' turn.

Ruth's numbers were excellent. He led the league with a .378 average, hit 46 homers and drove in 142 runs. (Washington's Goose Goslin had 5 more RBIs, costing Ruth the Triple Crown.) But the Senators' pitching, led by Walter "Big Train" Johnson, was the league's best. Perhaps the only solace for Ruth was watching McGraw lose another Series, albeit to the Sens, in seven games.

The ensuing offseason would nearly prove to be the undoing of baseball's greatest star.

Ruth was bored of domestic life and the farm where he lived with his first wife, Helen, and daughter, Dorothy. His winter of 1924–25 was "day and night, broads and booze," recalled teammate Joe Dugan in Creamer's *Babe*.

Usually, an offseason of gluttony would end when the Babe showed up in February at Hot Springs, Arkansas. There, he would usually get into shape before spring training and be ready for the start of the season. Not this time, as Ruth's marriage was falling apart and he apparently tried to make up for lost time.

A lesser mortal would have died. Ruth would work out during the day, then booze it up and eat voraciously and often be with a woman (or three) all night. Did I mention that he was battling the flu and a bad back at the same time? Finally, on a train on April 7, a week before Opening Day, Ruth collapsed and struck his head when he fell. He was incapacitated until June 1. By the time Ruth finally returned to the Yankee lineup, the team was 15-25, in seventh place, from which they would never recover.

Not that Ruth's season would get much better. Yankee manager Miller Huggins, whom Ruth never truly respected, saw that Ruth looked terrible and out of shape. In an effort to get him back to full strength, especially with the team playing terrible baseball, Huggins announced that he would try to give Ruth as much rest as he needed. Ruth took it as a rebuke and, on August 30, didn't show up for the game. Furious, Huggins fined him $5,000 (a record at the time) and suspended him indefinitely. Once again, Ruth miscalculated his own popularity. He called Huggins incompetent, blamed 1924 on his managing and gave the Yankees an "it's him or it's me" ultimatum.

Yankees' owner Jacob Ruppert responded by backing his manager, and Ruth meekly apologized. The damage had been done, and the Bombers finished 69-85, in fifth place. But as bad as the season was, as bad as Ruth had behaved, in the worst full season of his fifteen years in a Yankee uniform, he still posted a .290 batting average, .393 on-base percentage, .543 slugging percentage and .936 OPS. In 2018, Bryce Harper's .393 OBP was tenth best in the NL; Ruth's slugging and OPS would have placed him ninth and sixth, respectively.

There were many who thought Ruth's career was over after 1925. He was still only thirty-one but had abused his body to its limits. Few believed he had the self-discipline to return to being baseball's best and most popular player.

But he surprised everyone by dragging himself to Artie McGovern's gym in Manhattan and putting himself under his rigorous care: four-hour workouts and strict dieting. Ruth was transformed, going from 256 pounds to a svelte 212.

Ruth would train with McGovern for most of the rest of his career, and the results were evidence that he had (mostly) learned his lesson. He would hit 40 or more home runs for the next seven years, including 60 in 1927. For six of those years, he led the AL in home runs, slugging and OPS.

In 1932, at age thirty-seven, Ruth had his last Ruthian year, hitting .341 with 41 home runs, 137 RBIs, a .489 OBP and a 1.153 OPS. The Yankees would sweep the Cubs, and Ruth's legend would grow even bigger after his "called shot" in Game 3.

Ruth had done everything he wanted to do in baseball, save one; he wanted to manage. One would think that a man of Ruth's stature and winning pedigree would have been in great demand as a manager, despite his off-the-field reputation. The Yankees had two chances to hire Ruth as the skipper, the first in 1929 after the death of Miller Huggins. It seemed to many that Ruth should take over the club. Player-managers were common at that time; future Hall of Famers and Ruth contemporaries Ty Cobb, Tris Speaker, Eddie Collins and Rogers Hornsby had all done so. Yet, both Ruppert and, to a greater extent, Yankee GM Ed Barrow, were reluctant to give Ruth a chance. Though the Babe had calmed down substantially—his new wife, Claire Hodgson, now traveled with the team and kept a very close eye on his diet, wallet and, yes, the dames—Barrow felt it wouldn't work. Instead, they hired Ruth's teammate and pal Bob Shawkey to manage for 1930. It's just speculation on my part, but though Huggins and Ruth had been a solid partnership after the debacle of 1925, I suspect that Ruppert never really forgave Ruth for the years of insubordination under "Hug" and Barrow, who had managed Ruth in Boston in 1918 and found him to be a daily headache. Ruppert couldn't get past the bad memories.

Thanks to a two-year, $160,000 contract, Ruth was appeased and reluctantly accepted Shawkey's new role. However, when Shawkey was let go after a third-place finish and the Yankees hired Joe McCarthy to manage, Ruth was livid. McCarthy never played in the majors, he wasn't a Yankee and he was a National Leaguer.

Ruth didn't let his disappointment affect his play, but he held a grudge against Ruppert, Barrow and McCarthy until the day he died.

Jenkinson and the Babe's adopted daughter, Julia Stevens Ruth, both maintain that the main reason Ruth never got a chance to manage in the big leagues was that the establishment—mainly Judge Landis—feared that Ruth would get a job and try to integrate a roster.

There's no definitive proof of this, but, given his willingness to promote the Negro Leagues and the admiration he received from the black and brown communities of the time, is that hard to believe?

Jenkinson refers to the several interviews he did with Negro League veterans who played against Ruth, including Judy Johnson. "I had the privilege of becoming a personal friend to Judy Johnson....I originally met him to discuss legendary slugger Josh Gibson, but, over time, Mr. Johnson offered many unsolicited remarks about his admiration and affection for Babe Ruth. He articulated his passion for the Bambino as both a player and a human being. On the matter of Ruth's physical abilities, Johnson said,

'We could never seem to get him out no matter what we did.' In fact, in the sixteen games for which we have documentation, Babe went 25 for 54 with eleven home runs."

Babe was good friends with entertainer Bill "Bojangles" Robinson later in his career and made history in 1934 when he brought Robinson into the Yankee clubhouse as a guest, the first black man ever to do so. Robinson was an honorary pallbearer at Babe's 1948 funeral at St. Patrick's Cathedral.

Jenkinson offers this other tidbit:

> *When Ruth finally retired early in the 1935 season, he received countless offers to play exhibition games all over the country, including many in the New York area. With the exception of a police charity game in Minneapolis, he ignored them all until Sept. 29. What was the location that Babe Ruth chose for his first post-retirement "Big Apple" appearance? It was at Dyckman Oval in Harlem against the New York Cubans.*
>
> *In anticipation of the event, The Amsterdam News referred to Ruth as "The Great Man himself", and further stated, "as his popularity knew neither race, creed or color, the 'Oval' should present the most animated scene." That's exactly what happened. Over 8,000 fans, mostly folks of color, crammed into the little ballpark, while hundreds of others gathered on nearby rooftops. While rooting for a Cuban victory, they greeted Babe with warmth and affection.*

Perhaps Jenkinson is right. Perhaps the establishment felt that it wouldn't be able to control Ruth. Perhaps the Babe wanted to see the best players play, regardless of color or creed.

Either way, the Babe changed New York baseball forever.

6

CHRISTY MATHEWSON

[Christy] *Mathewson pitched against Cincinnati yesterday.*
Another way of putting it is that Cincinnati lost a game of baseball.
The first statement means the same as the second.
—Damon Runyon

I've talked about my love for baseball books, and another one of my favorites is *Greatest World Series Thrillers* by Ray Robinson. It's where I first read about Christy Mathewson. The chapter on Mathewson details his performance in the 1905 World Series: his 3 shutouts, giving up just 13 hits, striking out 18 and issuing just 1 walk over 27 innings.

In just the second World Series ever played, the best pitching performance ever took place.

That feat hasn't been equaled since. A few have come close. David Crawford Jones, in a special piece for MLB.com, ranked San Francisco Giant Madison Bumgarner's 2014 World Series as the best ever:

> *Had Madison Bumgarner never toed the rubber in Game 7 for the Giants against the Royals, his two victories earlier in the Fall Classic likely would have earned him Series MVP honors anyway. But in tossing five shutout innings on the road in Game 7, Bumgarner authored the most impressive relief performance in Fall Classic history.*
>
> *By the end, Kansas City had mustered just a .127 batting average off Bumgarner. Royals skipper Ned Yost described the experience as "hopeless."*

Great performance, for sure. But not better than Mathewson.

There is this gem from Bleacher Report's Andrew Gould: "Any modern pitcher who threw 27 scoreless innings would probably draw the No. 1 spot. However, Mathewson gets docked for playing in the segregated dead-ball era."

Mathewson dominated the best team in the American League, once on two days' rest, once on but one days' rest, so he doesn't get docked for anything unless you have an agenda.

During the 1850s, a saloon known as the Gotham was headquarters for the Gotham Base Ball Club. Much like today's premier baseball bar in New York City, Foley's NY, the Gotham was a showcase for the American Pastime, featuring a display behind the front bar of gilded trophy balls from victorious matches. The back bar featured a big gilt number 6 taken from the Americus Fire Company No. 6 (aka the "Big Six"), once voted the fastest fire company in the city.

I mention this for several reasons. First, the Gothams are still around today, albeit as part of a large group of Vintage "Base Ball" clubs that strive to follow the rules of the game as they existed in 1865. I had the pleasure of suiting up for the Gothams—my nickname was "Ink," in deference to my being a sportswriter—on more than one occasion, and *Gotham Baseball* sponsored the vintage baseball Gotham Cup tournament, which was played in Central Park in 2005–6.

Second, it was a Mathewson nickname—my personal favorite—the provenance of which goes back to Frank Graham's *The New York Giants: An Informal History of a Great Baseball Club.*

Perhaps award-winning sportswriter Mike Vaccaro, in his book *The First Fall Classic: The Red Sox, the Giants and the Cast of Players, Pugs and Politicos Who Re-Invented the World Series in 1912*, put it best when he wrote:

Christopher Mathewson—known as "Christy" or "Matty" to the common man; known as "Big Six" to teammate and opponent alike, though no one was ever quite sure why; referred to as "The Christian Gentleman" on the editorial pages of the nation's newspapers, which regularly espoused Mathewson as an ideal role model for both pie-eyed youth and weary citizen alike. Of course they knew the man who had won, to that very moment, 328 games, more than any pitcher who ever lived save for the great Cy Young (and even in 1912, Young's record of 511 career victories had been declared all but unapproachable), the man who had gained lasting fame tossing three shutouts at the Philadelphia Athletics in the 1905 World

Series, the man who embodied, along with his pugnacious manager John Joseph McGraw, the very spirit of the New York Giants, the flagship team of the National League, the pride of Manhattan, the obsession of composer George M. Cohan and Mayor William Jay Gaynor and ex-heavyweight champion James J. Corbett, to name three prominent acolytes.

I have always gravitated toward sportswriters who respect the history of the game, and Vaccaro is a great example. When I interviewed him for this book, I knew he'd be one of the few who could discuss historical and contemporary players with ease.

"Mathewson won 20 or more games 13 times. He won 30 or more four different times, including three years in a row from 1903 to 1905, then he won 37 more in 1908," said Vaccaro. "Back then, the Giants were what the Yankees would later become; the most famous team anywhere on the planet."

Mathewson was the biggest star on the biggest team. Perhaps more important, he was a—nay, *the*—symbol of "muscular Christianity" at a time when most ballplayers were considered profane louts (like Christy's manager and good friend John "Mugsy" McGraw).

"[He] was as perfect a model as anyone could ask for," said Vaccaro. "Not only was he a gifted athlete, but he also was a devout Christian, a loyal family man, his teammates and manager loved him, and the thing was, it wasn't an act."

Mathewson was the original Captain America.

In Philip Seib's 2003 book *The Player*, Mathewson is referred to as "the pitching marvel of the century," a Giant who "bestrode the field like a mighty Colossus." "Boys on sandlots imagined themselves as Christy Mathewson. Casual followers of baseball became more interested in checking the newspapers for reports about the young Giants pitcher. Stories about his pitching skills and gentlemanly character were told and retold. Mathewson had become a superstar."

He wasn't a flamethrower like Walter Johnson, but Christy's control was immaculate, and his out pitch was the fadeaway, which was essentially a screwball. Many historians estimate that Mathewson's velocity was around ninety to ninety-two miles per hour, hardly passable in today's game, especially for a big right-hander.

As Early Gustkey wrote in the *Los Angeles Times* on October 7, 1999, Mathewson's "greatest gift was pinpoint control and a faultless memory. Hitters often said that when they did manage a base hit off Mathewson, they never saw that same pitch in the same place again."

Baseball's "Christian Gentleman," Christy Mathewson. *Photo by The Baseball Hall of Fame.*

For Mathewson, as he wrote in his book *Pitching in a Pinch*, velocity was secondary to getting outs.

> *I have always been against a twirler pitching himself out, when there is no necessity for it, as so many youngsters do. They burn them through for eight innings and then, when the pinch comes, something is lacking. A pitcher must remember that there are eight other men in the game, drawing more or less salary to stop balls hit at them, and he must have confidence in them. Some pitchers will put all that they have on each ball. This is foolish for two reasons.*
>
> *In the first place, it exhausts the man physically and, when the pinch comes, he has not the strength to last it out. But second and more important, it shows the batters everything that he has, which is senseless. A man should always hold something in reserve, a surprise to spring when things get tight. If a pitcher has displayed his whole assortment to the batters in the early part of the game and has used all his speed and his fastest breaking curve, then, when the crisis comes, he "hasn't anything" to fall back on.*

Back then, baseball was more result oriented. So, Mathewson's goal was to last through a game, making sure his team won, which usually meant him not giving way to a lesser pitcher. It's what made him a great player and a valued teammate, as well as an extraordinary leader.

As the legend Damon Runyon wrote, Mathewson was more than just an ace, he was also the most important cog of the Giants, a role that McGraw needed him to be. "The mighty Mathewson was generally carrying a whole ball club on his back, and that ball club out in front, where it was most conspicuous. Time and time again it fell to him to fight the crucial battles of the big time outfit; to pitch the games on which hung the most important issues of the campaign, and he rarely failed."

One of the cooler things I came across while working on this chapter was a blog post from ESPN's Keith Olbermann in which he discussed the kind of pitcher Mathewson was. According to his research, and with a rare photo, Olbermann described Mathewson as a "drop and drive" hurler, much like Tom Seaver. In fact, according to a 2011 post on his *Baseball Nerd* blog, he sent the photo to Seaver himself. "There had been a lot of anecdotal evidence that Mathewson, who retired in 1916, had used a similar delivery [to Seaver]," said Olbermann. "But until the kind curators at the [Baseball Hall of Fame] photo archive let me look at their collection of glass images from the 1911 World Series, I don't think anybody had actually seen a game-action image of Mathewson."

In his book *The Art of Pitching*, Seaver ranks Mathewson the second-best pitcher of all-time, behind Walter Johnson. "There aren't a lot of people around anymore who can tell you what it was like to see him pitch, but the numbers Christy Mathewson left behind are staggering," said Seaver "They're not even something you can calculate in your mind. That's how good he was."

One way to determine just how dominant Mathewson's career was is to look at one of the more modern ways of measuring a pitcher's effectiveness: fielding independent pitching (FIP). According to MLB.com, "FIP is similar to ERA, but it focuses solely on the events a pitcher has the most control over—strikeouts, unintentional walks, hit-by-pitches, and home runs."

In his career (seventeen years), Mathewson's FIP is 2.26. It is fifth all-time and by far the best mark by a New York pitcher. His ERA is even lower: 2.13. And, yes, while he pitched during the segregated dead ball era, he was the best of the best of his time.

In 2007, Dave Studeman ranked Mathewson the fourth-best pitcher of all time, using Bill James's win shares above bench (WSAB). "WSAB takes a lot of things into account (ERA, wins, fielding support) to evaluate a pitcher and also applies a baseline that provides appropriate context.…It may not be perfect, but it's pretty darn good."

He was also one of the first five players elected to the National Baseball Hall of Fame in 1936.

"He had knowledge, judgment, perfect control and form," said Hall of Fame manager Connie Mack. "It was wonderful to watch him pitch—when he wasn't pitching against you."

So, from a traditional standpoint, Mathewson is fabulous. From a sabermetric standard, he's clearly worthy of his historical ranking.

On his Hall of Fame plaque, Christopher "Christy" Mathewson is called the "greatest of all the great pitchers in the 20th century's first quarter."

In my estimation, he's the greatest New York pitcher ever and our ace on the *Gotham Baseball* staff.

7

WHITEY FORD

If Edward Charles Ford was not the ideal Yankee, he will serve as the model until a better one comes along—if that be possible.
—Arthur Daley

For sixteen years, the left-hander known as Whitey Ford, wearing no. 16 on his back, was the best pitcher on the best team in baseball. The street-smart kid with the cobalt blue eyes and platinum blond hair was born in the Bronx, raised in Astoria, Queens, and a legend everywhere.

His catcher, Elston Howard, nicknamed the southpaw the "Chairman of the Board," due to his composure amid even the highest-pressure situations. Though blessed with the face of a cherub, the streetwise Ford was more of a Dead End Kid, which is probably why Yankee manager Casey Stengel dubbed his ace "Slick."

Thanks to the dads in his Astoria neighborhood, a thirteen-year-old Ford played his first real baseball with the 34th Avenue Boys, a club team made up of local kids that would stay together for several years. When it was time for high school ball, Ford's first choice was Bryant High School on 31st Avenue, but it didn't have a baseball team. So, Whitey went to the Manhattan School of Aviation Trades, which played its games under the Queensborough Bridge.

"I had a perfect attendance record at Aviation, but it was only because of baseball. I hated that school," Ford told Marty Appel in an article for the *New York Post* in 2000. "We were all supposed to become aircraft mechanics, and not one of us did."

Standing just five feet, nine inches tall and weighing in at about 150 pounds soaking wet, one of the greatest left-handed starters in the history of the game never had it easy. Maybe that's why from the get, Ford was money in big spots. Perhaps it was his self-confidence, and some might even say it was his being a "fresh kid." No matter how you want to categorize it, Cardinal great Dizzy Dean once said, "It ain't bragging if you can do it."

So, the little lefty playing ball under a bridge for an unknown school in the Northeast decided to write a letter to the New York Yankees about his ability. What happened next is the stuff of Hollywood, as told by SABR's Daniel R. Levitt:

> *Yankees scout Paul Krichell invited Whitey Ford to a tryout after the high-school lefty wrote him a letter. Ford was both a first baseman and pitcher, but at only 5-feet-6 Krichell recognized his limitations as a first baseman. He took Ford aside after the tryout and spent about 15 minutes working with him on a curveball. Krichell later remarked: "I gave him a few pointers so he wouldn't feel too bad about being turned down. We do that with all the kids who haven't got what it takes. If we can't make ballplayers out of them, we try to send 'em away as Yankee fans." Five months later Ford had grown and with Krichell's curve, he had developed into an excellent pitcher.*

The Boston Red Sox, then New York Giants and the Yankees offered Ford a contract to play pro ball after he graduated. C. Paul Rogers III, Ford's SABR biographer, wrote about how Ford became a Yankee.

> *Although Ford was hopeful of attracting a big bonus to sign as a professional, his size seemed to work against him. The Boston Red Sox first offered him $1,000 to sign after his championship game performance. The New York Giants then offered him $2,000, prompting the Red Sox to up their offer to $3,000. Ford most wanted to sign with the Yankees, and Paul Krichell soon called with an offer of $5,500. Ford verbally agreed and Krichell and another Yankee scout, Henry Hesse, traveled to Astoria to get Ford's signature on a contract and take him to an exhibition doubleheader in Queens involving some Yankee farmhands. They wanted Ford to sign right away, but Whitey said he preferred to sign when they brought him back after the games. While they were gone the Giants called, spoke to Ford's mother, and offered $6,500. Even though Ford would have signed with the Yankees for almost no bonus, it forced Krichell to up the Yankee offer to $7,000 on the spot.*

Seriously, how many of us would have taken the initial Red Sox offer? Or taken the chance to get the Yankees to up theirs? It paid off for Ford, he was a great investment for the Yankees, but the fans were the true beneficiary.

Ford began his professional baseball career in the Class-C Middle Atlantic League, going 13-4 with a 3.84 ERA and a 1.33 Walks and Hits Per Inning Pitched (WHIP) as an eighteen-year-old. He was promoted to Norfolk in the Class-B Piedmont League in 1948, dramatically improving his ERA (2.58 ERA) while his WHIP got worse (1.37).

When you rely on your stuff, rather than on velocity, you tend to get cute around the plate, and Ford would often walk more batters (113 that year) early in his career. However, he did lead the league in strikeouts (171) in 216 innings and complete games (16). It should also be noted that this was the first example of how well White could perform with a bigger workload.

In 1949, while pitching for the Binghamton Triplets, Ford finished at 16-5 with a 1.61 ERA and a 1.02 WHIP in just 168 innings (cutting his walks to 54). He was so pleased with his season that he called up "his old pal" Krichell and said he was ready for the big leagues.

"I wasn't being cocky," Ford told Bill Madden in the book *The Pride of October*. "It was in September and the Binghamton season was over and I still wanted to keep pitching and I really did think I belonged in the majors."

Krichell laughed but also let his boss, Yankee GM George Weiss, know that the Yankees had a good lefty who was on his way. Ford didn't make the team the following spring but got called up in late June as the Yankees were making a run at the pennant.

Handled carefully by manager Casey Stengel—a trend that would continue throughout Casey's tenure as Yankee skipper—the twenty-one-year-old rookie went 9-1 with a 2.81 ERA over 112 innings, a 20-game stretch that included 12 starts.

"When Whitey came up to us right around the All-Star break, you could see right away he was a confident kid who had ice water in his veins," Bobby Brown, the regular third baseman on that 1950 Yankee team, told Madden. "He had three pitches he could throw for strikes in tough spots and there was no stage fright in him."

Then came the Series. After the Yankees opened up a 3-0 lead over the Phillies, Stengel gave Ford the Game 4 start. Whitey responded by pitching eight scoreless innings en route to an eventual 5–2 win and his first World Series ring.

Then he got drafted.

He was assigned to the Signal Corps at Fort Monmouth, New Jersey, but after he fell off a couple of telephone poles during training, he was sent to the company commander, who told Ford his soldiering days would include pitching three days a week for the base's baseball team. Ford declined, thinking that kind of workload would affect his arm. He instead spent his two years in uniform playing on the side for the Monmouth Beach Tavern softball team to keep in shape.

While Whitey was away, the Yankees won two more World Series, beating Leo Durocher's Giants in 1951 and the "Boys of Summer" Brooklyn Dodgers in 1952. But Ford's return in 1953 probably played a big role in the team's return to the Fall Classic.

Though just twenty-four years old, Whitey stepped into the veteran rotation led by Vic Raschi (thirty-four), Eddie Lopat (thirty-five) and Johnny Sain (thirty-six) and led the team in wins (18), game starts (30), complete games (11), innings pitched (207) and strikeouts (110). Those totals had Ford in the top ten in the American League. However, he also led the team in walks (110), eighth-worst; he had the worst WHIP (1.45); and his FIP (4.00) was secondly only to veteran mop-up man Ray Scarborough.

Maybe because of the walks and Ford's relative inexperience, Stengel held him back in the Series, waiting until Game 4, with the Yankees leading the Series against Brooklyn, two games to one. Ford lasted just one inning, allowing three runs. Casey yanked him.

He fared much better in Game 6, allowing just one run and six hits while striking out seven over seven innings, but he did not figure into the eventual 4–3 win, which clinched the Series for the Yankees.

One wonders how much better Ford's career numbers would be if he'd had a different manager.

In his analysis on his wonderful blog *Cooperstown Cred*, Chris Bodig, a former producer for ESPN's *Baseball Tonight*, states the following:

> *From 1953-1960, Ford started only 42 games on 3 days of rest; 166 of his starts were on 4 days of rest or greater. It's for this reason that Ford never won 20 games during the Stengel years and ultimately why his career total of 236 wins is relatively paltry for a pitcher of his quality during the '50s and '60s.*

"Under Casey, I'd go five, even six days between starts," Ford told Madden. "I don't know why he did it that way. I just know my day to pitch was often a Monday, which was a traditional off-day in those days and I hated sitting in the dugout watching so many of those games when I thought I should have been pitching."

From 1956 to 1960, not much changed for Ford and the Yankees. They would win the World Series in 1956 and 1958 and pennants in '56, '57, '58 and '60. Ford won 72 games and averaged a 2.62 ERA, the two blips coming in 1947, when he was limited to just 129 innings because of a shoulder problem, and 1960, a World Series in which would be a turning point for the Yankees and Whitey Ford.

According to Mickey Mantle, as told to Mickey Herskowitz for their book *All My Octobers*:

> *The worst disappointment of my baseball career and one that hurts to this day was our loss to the Pittsburgh Pirates in the 1960 World Series. The better team lost, the only time I truly felt that way. It wasn't even close.*
>
> *We scored 55 runs, with 91 hits, 27 for extra bases, and still lost. I had my most productive Series ever, batting .400, hitting three homers, driving in 11 runs, and scoring eight. I even had a big hit when we rallied to tie the score with two runs in the ninth inning of the final game. But we still lost. Even now, 34 years later, I get upset when I think about it. The truth is, [manager] Casey Stengel blew it by not using (pitcher) Whitey Ford in the opener, which would have allowed him to start Whitey in three games. I didn't understand the decision then, and I still don't.*

The decision may have been based on sound baseball strategy. Art Ditmar, by 1960 data, had a slightly better season, winning three more games (15 to 12) and owning a slightly better ERA (3.06 to 3.08) during the regular season. Also, he was more of a groundball pitcher, which may have played a role as well. Throw in the fact that most of the 1960 Pirates' best hitters—Roberto Clemente, Dick Stuart and Don Hoak—were right-handed hitters, and you could make a case that the Ol' Perfesser knew what he was doing.

The only problem? Ditmar was no Whitey Ford, That became immediately apparent when the Pirates promptly knocked out Ditmar in the first inning of Game 1 and the Yankees lost the opener, 6–4. Ditmar was better in his Game 5 start: he lasted until the second inning of a 5–2 loss.

Whitey would pitch a complete-game shutout in both Games 3 and 6, but they were both blowouts, so Casey compounded the foolish decision to hold Whitey back by allowing him to stay in games the Yankees were way ahead in. So, there was no Slick coming out of the Forbes Field bullpen to save the day in Game 7. Instead it was Bill Mazerowski's moment, and the Pirates—not the Yankees—were World Champions.

Now, while the loss would always gall Yankees fans—and the team—it turned out to be the best thing that ever happened to Whitey Ford. Because, after the Series, Yankee owners Del Webb and Dan Topping forced out Stengel (as well as GM George Weiss, who was Stengel's biggest supporter in the organization) and hired the guy they really wanted in Ralph Houk.

Houk had been a rarely used third-string catcher for the Yankees from 1947 to 1954, serving as the de facto bullpen coach during his last two seasons in uniform. "I used to sit out there with pitchers who weren't in the starting rotation, and I learned exactly what went through their minds," said Houk, as quoted in his 2010 obituary in the *New York Times*.

In 1955, he accepted the job of manager of the team's Triple-A affiliate in Denver, and in 1957, he led the Bears to a Junior World Series championship. He became Stengel's first-base coach in 1958 and, by 1960, had attracted interest from other teams as a potential managerial candidate.

Houk, with new pitching coach Johnny Sain, believed that Ford would benefit from a bigger workload. Ford agreed. Predictably, in 1961, Whitey made a league-leading 39 starts and led the league with 25 wins and 283 innings pitched en route to winning the major-league Cy Young Award. (From 1956 to 1966, the award was given to the best pitcher in both the AL and NL.) In that season, Ford's best ever, three of his four losses were by scores of 2–1, 2–1 and 1–0. In the Series against the Reds, he extended his World Series shutout streak to 32 consecutive innings, which broke a record previously held by Babe Ruth.

Houk and Sain's plan worked out. From 1961 to 1965, Ford went 99-38 with a 2.85 ERA, 2.99 FIP and 1.16 WHIP. The Yankees won the 1961 and 1962 World Series. They won AL pennants in '63 and '64, losing the Series those two years in part because Ford finally showed signs of wearing down.

A combination of arm problems ended his career in 1967, but Ford's résumé for Cooperstown had been built: the highest winning percentage for any pitcher with at least 150 wins; a career ERA of 2.75; and World Series records for games started (22), innings pitched (146), wins (10) and strikeouts (94).

The consummate winner, maybe the best Yankee pitcher of all time, never lived the life of a superstar. "I once walked with him up Fifth Avenue from 42nd to 57th Street, fifteen blocks, and no one recognized him," Marty Appel told me. "Of course, lots of tourists in that stretch. I asked him if that was uncommon. He said he usually got recognized if

"The Chairman of the Board," Whitey Ford. *Photo by Bill Menzel.*

he was with Mickey. Otherwise, not. 'I'm an average-size, average-looking guy,' he said."

As of this writing, Whitey Ford is ninety years old and no longer does interviews. He lives quietly with his wife, Joan, and his absence at this year's Old-Timers' Day was felt all around Yankee Stadium. His name was announced, his photo was shown on the big scoreboard and he was saluted by the players and the crowd.

"He had an elegance about him on the mound, a regal presence," former player and broadcaster Tim McCarver told MLB.com's Anthony McCarron. "That made an impression, believe me."

As I close this chapter, I want to share my favorite Whitey quote, one that I think sums up how the greatest pitcher in Yankee history could walk down a Manhattan street and go unnoticed.

"What always used to piss Billy and Mickey off was we'd all go out partying and they'd get drunk and get into trouble but I never did," Ford once told Madden. "'But they didn't understand. I was a professional drinker. I grew up in a bar, which my father owned, a few blocks from one of the apartments we lived in Astoria. During my playing days, I spent a lot of time in Toots' joint, especially in the winter. We were great friends right to the end."

That sums up Whitey Ford perfectly. He was a consummate professional.

8

TOM SEAVER

Everything about Seaver was terrific. His arm, his delivery, his demeanor.
His personality, his knowledge....On a team that has almost nothing,
Tom Seaver had everything.
—John Feinstein

Every baseball fan I know has that one player they love above all else. For my dad, it was Duke Snider. My son Jack's was Jose Reyes. And for my cousin Dominick, it was Thurman Munson.

My all-time favorite is Tom Seaver.

I consider myself extremely fortunate to have interviewed Seaver a few times in my career, because once I started the process of writing this book in 2018, I was informed that Seaver would no longer do media interviews. "Tom can't do that kind of thing anymore," I was told. "And we'd appreciate it if you could keep that to yourself because the family isn't ready to announce anything yet."

A few months later, it became public: Seaver had dementia.

"Tom will continue to work in his beloved vineyard at his California home, but has chosen to completely retire from public life," the family said in the statement, released by the Baseball Hall of Fame. "The family is deeply appreciative of those who have supported Tom throughout his career, on and off the field, and who do so now by honoring his request for privacy."

In 2013, it was reported that Seaver was suffering from a recurrence of Lyme disease, first diagnosed in 1991. The relapse included cognitive problems similar to dementia. I didn't know how serious it was until I tried contacting him for an interview for this book.

I am ashamed to admit that, at first, I thought it was because the club was going to celebrate the fiftieth anniversary of the 1969 Mets in 2019 and that they were keeping "The Franchise" all to themselves.

I was so wrong.

I was a year old in 1969, so I clearly don't remember any of that year's incredible Fall Classic win over the heavily favored Baltimore Orioles. But to this day, I still feel like I watched every game. Because in many ways, I did. Before Netflix—heck, even before VHS—there was a thing called "World Series Films." My dad would often take me to events like Xaverian High School's Father & Son Sports Night, or a special Cub Scout event, at which someone would set up a projector and a screen, and the 1969 World Series film, narrated by Curt Gowdy, would be shown. You can get it on DVD, and it's so badass, they even got poor Ernie Banks—whose Cubs had just lost a contentious NL East race to the Mets—to be part of the folks exclaiming "They're Amazin!" montage to introduce the film.

Of course, my dad had been taking me to Mets games for as long as I can remember, and I had seen Seaver pitch at Shea Stadium. Pop always had a soft spot for Jerry Koosman, but Seaver was my guy. That drop-and-drive delivery, fluid mechanics—that's what a pitcher should look like.

I also had my dad's collection of Mets yearbooks, which I would read, over and over again.

In the 1966 yearbook, there's no mention of Seaver. The "How You Gonna Keep Em Down On the Farm?" page mentioned a young Derrel Harrelson (also known as Bud, who would be Seaver's roommate and slick-fielding shortstop on the 1969 Mets) as one of the "outstanding farm system prospects with bright Shea Stadium futures." But no Seaver.

However, in the 1967 revised yearbook, Seaver is the next-to-last player listed (on page 37), with a caption that reads, "Seaver The Saver: picked out of a hat."

Prophetic, that. Because he indeed was.

There are three photos as well, one of Seaver at his locker after his first win on April 20. Another is one of him pitching. The caption reads, "Camera catches training camp intensity that won him major league job after one year of pro ball."

That one year of pro ball was with the Triple-A Jacksonville Suns, a season that saw Seaver pitch 210 innings, post a 12-12 record with a 3.13

ERA and a 1.09 WHIP and average 8.1 strikeouts per nine innings. Also on that team was future World Series teammates Bud Harrelson, Ken Boswell and Tug McGraw. Both Tug and Seaver were just twenty-one; only Red Sox farmhand Billy Rohr (twenty) was younger in the International League that season.

Another teammate on the Suns was Bill Denehy, who shared a 1967 Topps rookie baseball card with Seaver. He, along with $100,000, was sent to the Washington Senators for the rights to manager Gil Hodges. Hodges, a former U.S. Marine like Seaver, would be the man Seaver said was the reason that 1969 was Amazin'.

But, really, it was Seaver the Saver who changed everything his rookie year in 1967. Like quite a few stories in this book, it was luck that made Seaver a Mets legend.

Seaver graduated from Fresno High School in 1962 and joined the Marines as a reservist. According to Seaver, the time he spent in boot camp prepared him for the major leagues. "I was 5 feet 10 and 165 pounds when I went into the Marines and 6-1 and 200 when I came out," said Seaver in a 1970 interview with the *New York Times*' Bill Surface in spring training. "My dad had already taught me to throw curves and sliders, but it didn't do me much good till then. With that extra weight, I could throw hard enough to get a baseball scholarship to college."

First at Fresno City College for two years, then two summer-ball stints with the Alaska Goldpanners, Seaver joined the legendary USC coach Rod Dedeaux in 1965 for his junior year. The only team that had scouted Seaver that season was the newly relocated Atlanta Braves, which signed him to a contract for $40,000 in February 1966.

Seaver, who had loved the Milwaukee Braves as a kid growing up in Fresno—Hank Aaron was his favorite player—didn't know that, by doing so, he had violated baseball's rules by signing while his college team's season was underway. (Seaver hadn't yet pitched in his senior year, but the Trojans had played two exhibition games.) Atlanta's blunder didn't only void the contract; it also cost Seaver his senior-year NCAA eligibility.

MLB commissioner William Eckert, perhaps motivated by a very angry Charles Seaver, who vowed to sue MLB for the blunder, ruled that any team that matched Atlanta's offer of $51,500 would participate in a lottery for Seaver's services.

At first, it didn't look remotely likely that the Mets would be interested. The team's president, George Weiss, had to be convinced by GM Bing Devine and farm director Joe McDonald that Seaver would be worth the expenditure. Weiss, who had helped build the Yankee dynasty, first as farm director for Ed Barrow beginning in 1932, then as GM from 1947 to 1960, had not had much success building the Mets from the ground up.

Finally, Weiss relented, and the Mets, along with the Philadelphia Phillies and Cleveland Indians, got the opportunity to pick Tom Seaver's name from a hat in March.

On April 1, 1966, Eckert pulled out the piece of paper that read "N.Y."

From 1962 to 1966, the Mets had been a joke. But their fans loved them anyway.

Everything was about to change for the ball club in Flushing.

"I hardly heard of the Mets much less wanted to play for them," Seaver told Surface. "But after I found out about them, it seemed like the quickest way to get to the big leagues."

A month later, Seaver signed with the Mets for a reported $50,000 bonus.

Though Seaver always gave credit to Hodges for setting the tone when the former Brooklyn Dodgers great became manager in 1968, it was a rookie Seaver in 1967 who changed everything.

"Seaver arrived in the spring of 1967 with thick thighs and a stocky butt and a wise head and excellent pitching mechanics and a cackling laugh about clubhouse pranks, but no sense of humor about losing," wrote George Vescey in the *New York Times*.

Up until that point, the Mets' best pitcher had been lefty Al Jackson, who had toiled for Casey Stengel, posting a 40-73 record with a very respectable 3.51 FIP for the worst team in the league from 1962 to 1965.

Seaver had little patience for the "lovable losers" tag. "When I came to the Mets, there was an aura of defeatism on the team; a feeling of let's get it over with. I could not accept that," he told *Sports Illustrated*'s William Legget. "Being brought up in California, I was unaware of the legend of 'Marvelous' Marv Throneberry. That lovable loser stuff was not funny to me. I noticed that the team seemed to play better when I pitched but, dammit, that wasn't right and I said so. I probably got a few people mad, but I went around and told the guys that if they did that for me and not for somebody else it was wrong. People pay money to see professional baseball played well and they put their emotions into it, too."

By July 11, thanks to an 8-5 record with a 2.65 ERA, Seaver was selected as an NL All-Star and got his first national spotlight when he finished the fifteenth inning of a 2–1 NL win at Anaheim Stadium, earning the save.

I asked Howie Rose, the long-tenured Mets broadcaster and fan of the team since his youth and the Mets inaugural season in 1962, what was so different about Seaver that it that made him The Franchise from the moment he stepped onto the Shea Stadium mound.

"Tom had discipline, respect for the game, respect for this craft, which he turned into an art as very few have ever done. And a desire to go far beyond where the Mets had ever been and settled for nothing resembling mediocrity," said Rose. "He treated every pitch as its own entity. Every pitch in his mind was either setting up the next one or potentially deciding what kind of a game it was going to be. He was calculated in his brilliance. He was a surgeon and was as cerebral a pitcher as has ever been on a mound. Then you factor in the natural talent and what he meant to the entire organization. He is its centerpiece."

In 2009, when the Mets celebrated the 1969 Series champions, I got to ask Seaver a bunch of questions, the first of which was about 1968. I had heard and read over the years that Seaver had always said that, while 1969 was special, it was the season before that set the tone. I also asked Tom if the fact that Gil had been a Marine and that Seaver had been a Marine had made the connection quicker.

"Sure," he said. "When he came over that year, he walked in and by his physical presence changed what was going on. Immediately. Then he spoke and it changed even more."

The *New York Times'* Michael Powell pointed out in his "Sports of The Times" column that, in 1969, in a year when Seaver went 25-7 with a 2.21 ERA, "he pitched in the ninth inning 17 times and surrendered not a single run. Oh, yes, in September of that year, he went 6-0 with an 0.83 ERA."

After winning the Series, the Mets had identical 83-79 records in 1970 and 1971. The Roberto Clemente/Willie Stargell Pirates won the division both years. Seaver was Seaver, posting an NL-best 2.82 ERA in 1970, along with a league-leading 283 strikeouts. He was even better in 1971, again leading the NL in several categories—1.76 ERA, 289 Ks, 0.946 WHIP—yet he finished second in the Cy Young Award voting to Ferguson Jenkins.

In 1972, Hodges died of a heart attack right before the season was scheduled to start, and while Seaver had another stellar season (21-12, 2.92 ERA, 1.12 WHIP), the Mets couldn't manage more than 83 wins for a third straight season, and the team hit an NL-worst .225.

Seaver's second Cy Young Award led the Mets to a pennant in 1973, but manager Yogi Berra—who had replaced Hodges in 1972—opted to go for the knockout punch in Game Six, letting Seaver face the A's on three days' rest. Seaver held the A's to just two runs over seven innings, but the Mets

There are few things in baseball more perfect than a Tom Seaver windup. *Photo by the Baseball Hall of Fame.*

couldn't muster an offense that day, and Oakland went on to win in seven games, the first of their three straight World Series victories.

Seaver suffered through a terrible (for him) 1974 season (11-11, 3.20 ERA), dealing with hip and arm issues. Before the season, he had threatened to hold out in spring training but eventually signed for $140,000, the highest salary for a pitcher in all of baseball. The loss of Hodges, on an emotional and baseball level, was starting to be felt throughout the organization, and the team stumbled to 71-91.

The next season would be better for Seaver. He came roaring back with his third Cy Young Award (22-9 with a 2.38 ERA and a league-leading 243 strikeouts). But 1975 was perhaps the true beginning of the end for Seaver and the Mets.

Through Joe McDonald, who had been promoted from farm director to GM at the start of the season, M. Donald Grant's destruction of the

Amazin's had begun. Bad trades, pursuit of bargain-basement free agents and the forcing of several not-yet-ready-for-prime-time players to replace injured players prevented a team with a top three of Seaver, Koosman and Jon Matlack from reaching its potential.

Seaver's frustration with the team's direction and other MLB stars' new contracts (like Jim "Catfish" Hunter's five-year, $3.75-million contract with the New York Yankees) wasn't based solely on money. Seaver wanted the Mets to be players in the mix for the unfolding free agent market.

But the Mets' owner and biggest fan, Joan Payson, died in December 1975, and the team was run by Grant, because her children and Payson's husband had no desire to.

Grant was now intent on running the show.

"He was a stockbroker who didn't know beans about baseball," said Whitey Herzog, whom I met at a spring training minor-league baseball game in Tampa in 2008. Herzog was a great baseball mind who helped build the 1969 Mets (and later became a Hall of Fame manager) but eventually was forced out because Grant felt he was insubordinate.

During the owners' lockout in the spring of 1976, Seaver took a leadership role as a union rep, and Grant was incensed. In a wonderful piece written for *Harper's* following the trade, A. Bartlett Giamatti—who would later become the commissioner of baseball—wrote: "[Grant thought] Tom wanted too much. Tom wanted, somehow, to cross the line between employee and equal, hired hand and golf partner, 'boy' and man. What M. Donald Grant could not abide—after all, could he, Grant, ever become a Payson? Of course not. Everything is ordered. Doesn't anyone understand anything anymore?"

Seaver was vocal about his contract, yes. But he also wanted the team to be the best that it could be. "The money was always secondary to my loyalty to the Mets," Seaver told *Sports Illustrated's* Kent Hannon in 1977. "The people who think I was bitter about not making more money or who think I was trying to force a trade by asking that my contract be renegotiated won't believe me. But for the record, my loyalty to the Mets and my desire to make them competitive always came first. I don't think I've shown myself to be a greedy person."

In the end, with the help of a number of caustic columns by Dick Young—whose son-in-law Thornton Geary was working for the Mets—Seaver demanded a trade and was sent to the Reds. We all know what happened after.

"With him, it was a matter of loyalty," Nancy Seaver told *Sports Illustrated's* Frank DeFord in 1981, referring to the "Midnight Massacre" deal that sent

Seaver to Cincinnati. "And his loyalty was thrown into his face. Tom was hurt badly. I don't think, even now, he'd like to admit how much. He wanted to live and die at [Shea Stadium]. And they jilted him."

Incomprehensibly, it would happen again.

In my mind, Tom Seaver's triumphant return to the Mets in 1983 was a dream come true.

I followed his career with the Reds, but mostly through box scores, *Sports Illustrated* and the *Game of the Week*. I never thought I'd see Tom in blue and orange again. But it happened.

Opening Day 1983 at Shea Stadium. I remember it as colorful as the moment when black-and-white Dorothy Gale first peeked outside the door at the full-color Land of Oz.

In truth, I watched Opening Day at Shea Stadium in 1983 on a twelve-inch black-and-white TV my dad had reclaimed on his New York City Department of Sanitation route. But I remember it in full color, not truly believing it was really happening. The roar of the crowd when PA announcer Jack Franchetti said, "Batting ninth and pitching, now warming up in the bullpen, Number 41."

The best player to ever wear the orange and blue was back, and all that was good was so again. He struck out Pete Rose (whom I disliked immensely) to start the game, and the cheers were even louder.

It wouldn't be a banner year for the Mets. They would finish 68-94 and manager George Bamberger would quit in June, but they would also get Keith Hernandez later that month in a trade, and Darryl Strawberry made his debut, winning Rookie of the Year.

Go search YouTube for some of Hernandez's top plays when he joined the Mets. A couple are fantastic plays where he ranges far to his right and makes a great throw to a hustling Seaver to make the play at first.

Seaver's record was just 9-14, but at age thirty-eight, he still led the team in innings pitched (231), ERA (3.55), FIP (3.77) and WHIP (1.24).

At the start of the season, Frank Cashen, the man who had traded Charlie Puleo and two minor leaguers to get Seaver back, told reporters, "What we want is a senior pitcher who can serve as a role model for our younger players."

So, why in God's name did the Mets—who had finally brought back the prodigal son—let him be selected by the White Sox in the free agent compensation draft after the season?

Nelson Doubleday said he was "devastated" by the loss of Seaver just one year after the Mets had brought him back to New York, presumably to finish his career. Doubleday, who did not deal with the day-to-day operations of the team, likely didn't know that it was even a possibility.

Fred Wilpon was a minority owner in 1983, but as team president, he was very involved. Perhaps he and GM Cashen were surprised that the White Sox—the only team that would get a pick in the pool—decided to pick Seaver.

"Mea culpa, mea culpa, mea maxima culpa. I had the final decision, I made a mistake. We made a calculated and regrettable gamble," said Cashen.

A mistake?

Howie Rose said the decision to leave Seaver unprotected was unforgivable and may have cost the Mets dearly in the long run.

"Tom would have been happy to finish his career as a Met, that's why he came back. That's why he agreed to the trade," said Rose, who added that, as a "10 and 5 player," Seaver had to agree to the trade for it to go through.

> *I would submit that it was the most indefensible act of a Mets front office executive in the franchise's history. We could talk all you want about the Nolan Ryan trade or any other trade that didn't work out. But that is, you know, that was the most calculated miscalculation. And I know I say that somewhat cynically, but that was just indefensible on any level. And I can make the case that it might have cost the Mets a pennant or two because I believe Seaver won 31 games over the next two years for the White Sox. Do you think he might have made a difference in '84 and '85? Especially with that young pitching staff here? I would say that that was the worst blunder—at least from an administrative standpoint, not a qualitative perspective—ever made.*

It was refreshing to hear Howie say that, because I've always felt the same way.

It's my feeling that Davey Johnson, whom I admire and respect, didn't want to have an influential veteran like Seaver around. I also contend that Cashen, who hired Davey on October 13, 1983, agreed to make it happen.

Among the players the Mets protected instead of Seaver? Thirty-two-year-old and injury-prone Craig Swan, coming off a terrible 1983 season (2-8 with a 5.51 ERA). Davey would cut Swan by May 9 the next year.

Wilpon, who conveniently was a good friend of White Sox owner Jerry Reinsdorf, certainly could have suggested the White Sox might benefit from having a guy like Seaver around.

Do I have any on-the-record confirmation of this? I do not.

All I can offer is this: On December 14, 1982, the *New York Times*' Dave Anderson quoted Seaver—who was about to rejoin the Mets—as saying, "looking to the future, I think I would like to run a ball club in the front office or manage on the field." In the column, Anderson called Seaver, once he decided to retire, the next manager of the Mets.

In 1985, with the Mets trying to get past the Cardinals in the NL East, Cashen told Davey Johnson that he had a chance to get Seaver, and Davey said no. That's according to Davey's book *Bats*, in which he notes that Cashen told him that Seaver was available, and the Mets' manager didn't want the pitcher who had once been the "franchise" at Shea Stadium.

When told about the passage in Davey's book, Seaver told the *New York Times* he wasn't surprised. "I've heard from other sources that Davey wasn't too hot about having me around."

Hindsight is 20-20, as they say, but maybe a pitcher like Dwight Gooden could have benefited by having a legend like Tom Seaver around, because, according to Tony LaRussa, it certainly helped the White Sox.

"We didn't know if he would act like he was Tom Seaver, act like he deserved to be treated like he was Tom Seaver," White Sox manager LaRussa told the *Chicago Tribune* in the spring of 1985. "His attitude was perfect. His record and reputation meant nothing compared to the team good. He puts that first. For me to just write his name on the lineup card is an honor for a manager."

In 1984, Seaver went 15-11 with a 3.95 ERA, 236 IP and a 1.17 WHIP, which would have placed him second in wins and WHIP to Gooden and first in innings. The Mets finished second in the NL East, six games behind the Cubs.

Good thing they protected Swan.

In 1985, Tom was even better, 16-11 with a 3.17 ERA, 238 IP and a 1.22 WHIP. New York lost the NL East by three games to the St. Louis Cardinals. Think he would have been a better option in the rotation than Ed Lynch? (Sorry, Ed, I love ya, but c'mon.)

Whether it was on purpose or by stupidity, the fact that Tom Seaver won his 300th game in Yankee Stadium dressed in the pajamas the White Sox called uniforms has always been an *infamnia* to me. I was overjoyed for him personally, because I loved the guy, but especially because it was during a pennant race for the Yankees.

Yankee Stadium erupted with joy, but the Boss was none too happy.

"I'm happy for Tom and proud of him, but I wanted to beat him so bad today. I don't know if it bothered our players to lose—I think it bothered

The 1950s-era Home uniform. *Design and photo by Todd Radom.*

The 1950s-era Road uniform. *Design and photo by Todd Radom.*

The 1970s-era Home uniform. *Design and photo by Todd Radom.*

The 1970s-era Road uniform. *Design and photo by Todd Radom.*

The Modern-era Home uniform. *Design and photo by Todd Radom.*

The Modern-era Road uniform. *Design and photo by Todd Radom.*

Above: Monte Irvin, Left Field. *Illustration by John Pennisi. Uniform design by Todd Radom.*

Opposite, top: Willie Mays, Center Field. *Illustration by John Pennisi. Uniform design by Todd Radom.*

Opposite, bottom: Babe Ruth, Right Field. *Illustration by John Pennisi. Uniform design by Todd Radom.*

Above: Christy Mathewson, Right-Handed Starting Pitcher. *Illustration by John Pennisi. Uniform design by Todd Radom.*

Opposite, top: Whitey Ford, Left-Handed Starting Pitcher. *Illustration by John Pennisi. Uniform design by Todd Radom.*

Opposite, bottom: Tom Seaver, Right-Handed Starting Pitcher. *Illustration by John Pennisi. Uniform design by Todd Radom.*

Carl Hubbell, Left-Handed Starting Pitcher. *Illustration by John Pennisi.*
Uniform design by Todd Radom.

Dazzy Vance, Right-Handed Starting Pitcher. *Illustration by John Pennisi. Uniform design by Todd Radom.*

Mike Piazza, Catcher. *Illustration by John Pennisi. Uniform design by Todd Radom.*

Lou Gehrig, First Baseman. *Illustration by John Pennisi. Uniform design by Todd Radom.*

Jackie Robinson, Second Baseman. *Illustration by John Pennisi.*
Uniform design by Todd Radom.

Derek Jeter, Shortstop. *Illustration by John Pennisi. Uniform design by Todd Radom.*

David Wright, Third Baseman. *Illustration by John Pennisi. Uniform design by Todd Radom.*

Mariano Rivera, Closer. *Illustration by John Pennisi. Uniform design by Todd Radom.*

Joe Torre, Manager. *Illustration by John Pennisi. Uniform design by Todd Radom.*

some of them—but it sure bothered the hell out of Billy and me," Yankees owner George Steinbrenner told the *New York Times*' Michael Martinez. "You've got to want to be the right part of history, and we weren't."

Despite the bluster, it was classy for the Yankees to invite original Met broadcaster Lindsey Nelson to call the final moments of Seaver's 300th. That made it almost bearable, but it was much like watching Seaver throw his only no-hitter in a Reds uniform.

Tom Seaver would have his day at Shea on July 24, 1988. The legendary Bob Murphy and his broadcast partner and Hall of Famer Ralph Kinner were the masters of ceremonies for Tom Seaver Day. They introduced Seaver, who then addressed the crowd. "If my number was ever retired, there would be one way I want to say thank you…to everyone here on the field, to everyone in the stands, to everyone at home watching on television," said Seaver. "If you would just allow me one moment, I'm going to say thank you in my own special way. If you know me, how much I love pitching, you'll know what this means to me."

He then sprinted to the mound he once called home and proceeded to take a bow of gratitude to every section of the stadium.

The team he made champions may never have appreciated him the right way, but Tom Seaver has always known how much every one of us love him.

It's too bad that this chapter has taken on a bit of an angry tone, because I love Tom Seaver. However, I know I speak for many Met fans that are just as upset with how the team has treated The Franchise, especially now.

There are plans for a statue, and the new address for Citi Field is 41 Seaver Way. But, frankly, it's a day late and a dollar short for most. "The Mets missed a huge opportunity to give Seaver his proper due when they opened Citi Field in 2009," Nick Duinte wrote for *Forbes* in 2019. "Seaver could have enjoyed his monument in-person alongside his family in the city where he built his legend."

Seaver deserved better. But I don't want to end on such a somber note.

"Tom Terrific" will always be "The Franchise." *Photo by Bill Menzel.*

On Opening Night of Citi Field in 2009, Seaver was in the press box taking some questions. I asked him what he liked most about the new ballpark.

"The dirt," said Seaver, which caused some laughter. But he was serious and went on. "It's really special. I wish we would have had that quality of dirt on the Shea infield."

A few minutes later, Mets starter Mike Pelfrey slipped on the mound. "So much for your dirt." I cracked. Seaver glared at me for a second, and then he chuckled.

After so many years of joy he provided me and countless other fans, making Tom Terrific smile for a moment was a thrill I'll never forget.

9

CARL HUBBELL

If I had a ball game to be pitched and my life hung on the balance,
I'd want Carl Hubbell to pitch it.
—Red Barber

The first time I heard the name Carl Hubbell was during the 1984 All-Star Game, when rookie Dwight Gooden of the New York Mets and Fernando Valenzuela of the Dodgers combined for six straight strikeouts, the All-Star record.

During the broadcast, it was mentioned that, fifty years earlier, at the first-ever All-Star Game—1934 at Wrigley Field—Hubbell struck out Babe Ruth, Lou Gehrig, Jimmie Foxx, Al Simmons and Joe Cronin in succession.

Cronin's pitch was called a reverse-curve, a descendant of Christy Mathewson's fadeaway, but it became known as the screwball as we know it today. When "Big Six" used the fadeaway, he used it just a few times a game. "Many persons have asked me why I do not use my 'fade-away' oftener when it is so effective," wrote Mathewson in *Pitching in a Pinch*. "The only answer is that every time I throw the 'fade-away' it takes so much out of my arm. It is a very hard ball to deliver. Pitching it ten or twelve times in a game kills my arm, so I save it for the pinches."

Hubbell's screwball was faster and used more often, and it was the pitch that made him a Hall of Famer. But it wasn't an easy road to Cooperstown.

To begin with, Mathewson's commentary on the fadeaway in 1912 likely resonated throughout the game, as his influence was legendary. In 1922, following his graduation from high school, Hubbell had not pitched well enough as a high schooler to attract big-league scouts, but he got his chance to play pro ball when he signed on as a low-level minor leaguer in the Oklahoma State League.

According to Hubbell's SABR biographer and author Fred Stein, to gain an edge, Hubbell developed his screwball by 1925. "At 22, the lefthander had a 17-13 season with Oklahoma City of the Western League," wrote Stein. "By this time, Hubbell's reverse-curve screwball was part of his pitching repertoire. He had come upon the pitch in attempting to turn the ball over in order to make it sink."

According to MLB historian John Thorn:

> [In Oklahoma] *Hubbell met an older pitcher named Lefty Thomas who worked with him on developing a sinker. As Hubbell tinkered with the new delivery he kept turning his wrist farther and farther over, and as he did, he developed an entirely new pitch—the screwball. Christy Mathewson had thrown a "fadeaway," a changeup with a reverse break, but Hubbell threw his pitch hard—so hard and so often that when his career was done, his left arm turned inward.*

The Detroit Tigers thought enough of Hubbell to purchase his contract in 1926, but in the left-hander's first training camp, the screwball he had developed to turn him into a real prospect nearly doomed his career.

Author Lang Leave once wrote, "You can create something that is pure genius, but you have to get your timing right." In Hubbell's case, this rings particularly true.

Spring training 1926: The Tigers manager is Ty Cobb, the same Cobb who would be inducted into the inaugural class of the Baseball Hall of Fame in 1936 with Mathewson, Walter Johnson, Babe Ruth and Honus Wagner. It is likely that Cobb remembered Mathewson's words, or at least held the belief that the screwball was bad for the arm, because he forbade Hubbell to throw the pitch.

Years later, former Tiger pitcher Bill Moore told author Richard Bak (*Cobb Would Have Caught It: The Golden Age of Baseball in Detroit*) that he recalled Cobb approaching Hubbell at camp. "Carl Hubbell was in the Tigers' farm system at the same time I was," recounted Moore. "Carl and I knew each other. We pitched against each other in the International League. Later, of course, he had all those great years with the Giants. Threw that screwball, you know. That was his bread-and-butter pitch. You know what Cobb told him to do with it? 'Get rid of that damn pitch.'"

For two years, robbed of his best pitch, Hubbell slumped, first in Triple-A Toronto in 1926. Then he was demoted to Class-B ball, where he pitched well (14-7). But the Tigers had seen enough, selling him to Beaumont in the Texas League.

Moore said Hubbell told him, "The best thing that ever happened to me was when that son of a bitch [Cobb] released me."

Enter John "Mugsy" McGraw.

Remember that whole timing thing? New York Giant scout Dick Kinsella (no relation to *Shoeless Joe* author W.P. Kinsella—I looked it up) also happened to be a delegate to the Democratic National Convention in Houston and took in a Texas League game, which just happened to be one in which Hubbell was impressive, as he had been throwing his screwball again.

As recounted by Frank Graham in *The New York Giants*, Kinsella warned McGraw that while the twenty-five-year-old left-hander had been impressive, he threw a screwball.

McGraw, who apparently hadn't read *Pitching in a Pinch*, replied that his star Mathewson had thrown a fadeaway and "it never hurt his arm" and instructed Kinsella to pay $30,000 for the rights to Hubbell, which was then a record for the Texas League.

Under McGraw, Hubbell became a reliable starter, from 1928 to 1932 averaging 15 wins, 8 losses and a 3.11 ERA. In 1932, McGraw retired from managing after the team started 17-23, and first baseman Bill Terry took over the team.

McGraw had given Hubbell his shot and had been a calming force during his rookie season, but it was under Terry that Hubbell became the best pitcher in baseball.

In a 1982 oral interview with Carl Hubbell conducted by SABR's Oral History committee, Hubbell discussed the good and bad of McGraw.

I'd had such a bad experience in Detroit. [McGraw] *gave me a chance to pitch in the big leagues, and I appreciate it a hell of a lot. But he called every pitch, and every pitch was a breaking ball, be a curveball or a screwball. He didn't think you had sense enough to throw a fastball. He must have been the worst curveball hitter in the world....He give me a chance to pitch. I didn't want to say anything* [bad about him]. *Four years with him, it's a wonder my arm lasted as long as it did, it really is.*

Hubbell finished the 1932 season with an 18-11 record, a 2.50 ERA and a league-best 1.056 WHIP. He equaled his then-career high of 18 wins, and his ERA and WHIP were his best to date.

Hubbell was crowned "King Carl" in 1933, a season about which MLB.com's Will Leitch said, "numbers are sometimes so impressive they seem to come from a different sport altogether."

Hubbell went 23-12 with a 1.66 ERA over 308 innings. The wins, ERA and IP led the league, as did his minuscule 0.982 WHIP. Those numbers earned him the NL MVP. The Giants, picked by many experts to finish sixth in the eight-team National League to start the season, won the pennant, and Hubbell punctuated his season by going 2-0 in the World Series, posting a 0.00 ERA over 20 innings.

It was the start of a five-season stretch (1933–37) in which the "Meal Ticket" would post a 115-50 record with a 1.09 ERA while averaging 298 innings a season.

Hubbell would post another MVP season in 1936, with the screwballer going 26-6 with a league-leading 2.31 ERA and a 1.05 WHIP. He went 16-0 in his last 16 starts (and would win his first 8 starts in 1937 for a record 24-game winning streak, which still stands). He pitched well in the World Series that year against the Yankees of DiMaggio, Gehrig and Bill Dickey, but the Giants lost.

The next season would be Hubbell's last great campaign.

According to Warren Corbett, in an article for SABR.org titled "Hubbell's Elbow: Don't Blame the Screwball," it was during 1937 spring training that Hubbell got his enduring "Meal Ticket" nickname.

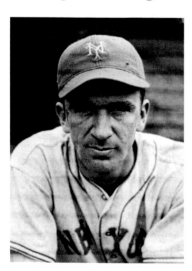

Carl Hubbell, the "Meal Ticket."
Photo by The Baseball Hall of Fame.

"The Cincinnati manager Charlie Dressen was quoted as saying, 'Hubbell is Terry's meal ticket, and when Hubbell is through so is Terry.' Dressen protested that he didn't say it—it was Brooklyn manager Burleigh Grimes. Whoever the author, the name stuck."

Dressen would also utter the infamous "The Giants is dead" as manager of the Brooklyn Dodgers who would blow the 1951 pennant. In this case, he was correct. Hubbell and the Giants would lose the Series that year and the following year (1937), and the 1938 season began the final stretch of the southpaw's career.

He would remain a more than serviceable pitcher, going 61-52 with a 3.51 ERA, but he was no longer dominant. Hubbell's elbow gave out early in 1943, and he retired with a 4-4 record, the only time in his sixteen seasons that he won fewer than 11 games.

Throwing the screwball those years left its mark, deforming his left arm; when it was at rest, his palm faced outward instead of in. "I couldn't get over Hubbell's hand," writer Roger Angell observed in his wonderful *Season Ticket: A Baseball Companion*. "It was like meeting a gladiator who bore scars inflicted at the Colosseum."

After he retired, Hubbell was named the Giants' farm director, a job he would hold for more than thirty years. Under his direction, the Giants' system produced players Willie Mays, Orlando Cepeda, Willie McCovey, Juan Marichal and Gaylord Perry. This was no charity gig. According to the *San Francisco Examiner*, Hubbell "made all decisions on which prospects the Giants would draft and which of the organization's minor-league players got promotions."

In 1977, a stroke forced Hubbell's retirement from his post as farm director. He then became a scout, a post he held until his death at eighty-five on November 21, 1988, from injuries suffered in a car accident.

Before his death, Hubbell spoke with George Vescey from the *New York Times* about his famous screwball and about then-phenom Fernando Valenzuela.

> *"He holds the ball exactly the way I did," said Hubbell. "Other pitchers slide it off the side of their hand, but that's not the real good screwball. He's got the same motion, the same grip, each time. If you don't do that, the hitters will soon detect it."*
>
> *When Valenzuela burst into prominence in 1981, his manager, Tom Lasorda, told writers: "There's an old left-hander out on the desert who used to throw a pretty good screwball. You ought to call him if you want to know about the screwball."*
>
> *Hubbell says with a chuckle: "I got more attention from Fernando than when I was pitching. They'd ask me the darndest things. Sometimes they'd ask: 'Was it something you put on the ball?' And I'd tell them, 'Yeah, I put something on the ball: three fingers.' I never became famous for the screwball until Valenzuela came along."*

The 1984 All-Star Game, played at San Francisco's Candlestick Park, marked the fiftieth anniversary of Hubbell's legendary 1934 All-Star Game performance. Before he got to witness Valenzuela and Gooden match his feat from fifty years earlier, Hubbell threw out the ceremonial first pitch.

It was a screwball.

10

DAZZY VANCE

When the greatest of all Brooklyn pitchers was fogging them over for the Dodgers, the right sleeve of his sweatshirt was an unsightly rag, a flapping thing of shreds and tatters. Daz would hide the ball until the last instant and then if the batter was lucky, he would see something white rocketing toward him out of a distracting flutter of dry goods.
—Red Smith

One of the tougher decisions when compiling the Gotham Baseball Legends team was the last rotation spot. As I mentioned earlier in this book, the final spots were chosen by yours truly, but I only did so after talking to many folks whose baseball opinions mattered to me.

For starters (see what I did there?), the right-handed rotation ballot results (over ten thousand folks voted) looked like this:

Player	Team	Vote %
Tom Seaver	**Mets**	**53.2**
Dwight Gooden	Mets	21.06
Don Newcombe	Dodgers	1.73
Dazzy Vance	Dodgers	0.17
Red Ruffing	Yankees	0.28
Mel Stottlemyre	Yankees	0.61
Christy Mathewson	**Giants**	**22.45**
Joe McGinnity	Giants	0.0

The left-hander results are as follows:

Player	Team	Vote %
Carl Hubbell	Giants	16.14
Art Nehf	Giants	0.17
Whitey Ford	**Yankees**	**40.37**
Lefty Gomez	Yankees	5.89
Johnny Podres	Dodgers	2.72
Rube Marquard	Dodgers	0.34
Jerry Koosman	**Mets**	**25.88**
Sid Fernandez	Mets	6.85

As you can see, Jerry Koosman was voted over Carl Hubbell for the second left-hander spot, which was clearly (in my mind) unfair. So, once I decided on Hubbell, I focused on the also-rans, as well as those who didn't make the ballot for the final spot.

First, I pooled my "panel" of baseball experts and historians for their opinions. For one, Marty Appel was shocked that Red Ruffing wasn't on the final staff. "Ruffing won 231 games for the Yankees, he's the winningest right-hander in Yankee history, he's got to be there, no?" he asked. "Look at his World Series numbers!"

For the record, Ruffing's Series numbers are really impressive: 7-2, 2.63 ERA in 10 games. It was hard to leave Ruffing off, but his career WHIP (1.29) and FIP (3.86), while certainly impressive, weren't nearly as impressive as those of some of the other candidates.

The ballot results made me consider Koosman for the fifth starter, but as impressive as his career was (1.25 WHIP) and (3.26 FIP), he came up short in comparison to another former Met, David Cone.

Coney was an intriguing candidate who didn't make the ballot, but he's as Gotham Baseball as they come. In his seven seasons as a Met, during a far better era for hitters, Cone's pitching peripherals (1.192 WHIP, 2.98 FIP) were outstanding. I also loved that Cone also became a key starter for the Yankees' last dynasty (and maybe the last dynasty of its kind). That kind of relevancy might have made for a cool crossover candidate.

But how could I add Cone when Dwight Gooden, whose career WHIP (1.18) and FIP (2.77) as a Met right-hander were even better than Cone's? I adored Gooden and had a front-row seat (right behind home plate) to witness him strike out 16 Giants at Shea Stadium on August 20, 1985.

Above: Yankee historian and best-selling author Marty Appel says Red Ruffing should be a Gotham Baseball Legend. I respectfully disagree. *Photo by The Baseball Hall of Fame.*

Left: Brooklyn fans hated Sal Maglie until he helped the team win a pennant in 1956. *Illustration by John Pennisi.*

But while I would have loved to add another Met to this staff, for obvious reasons, would it be the right thing to do?

I kept looking.

As good as the pitchers I mention here are, none of them ever dominated at the level of Mathewson, Seaver, Ford and Hubbell. The final spot came between the two who did. One was so scary they called him a demon; the other was a guy who most people have never heard of.

Though he signed his first professional contract at twenty-one, Sal Maglie wouldn't get a real shot at sticking in the major leagues until he was a grizzled thirty-three-year-old. There were lots of reasons for that, and I suggest you read Judith Testa's excellent *Sal Maglie: Baseball's Demon Barber* (Northern Illinois University Press, 2007) to get the whole story.

Suffice it to say, from 1950 to 1952, he would be one of the most dominant—and most feared—pitchers in all of baseball. Acclaimed writer Robert Creamer, who chronicled Maglie in *Sports Illustrated* in 1951, put it best:

> [Maglie] *hovers over the Borough of Brooklyn like the angel of darkness. Small children are cowed into obedience by the mention of its name, strong men pale and women weep. "The Barber?" the Brooklyn Dodger fan asks fearfully, looking over his shoulder. "Is he pitching tonight? We never beat him. Never."*
>
> *This is legend, of course. Salvatore Anthony Maglie of the New York Giants (for indeed it is he) never scared a child to sleep, never made a woman weep and never beat the Dodgers every time he faced them, although his margin of superiority—23 victories over Brooklyn to only 10 defeats—is remarkable. But his undeniable effectiveness, his grim shadowy appearance, his obvious relish of the challenging job facing him each time he pitches against Brooklyn, have given him an aura of invincibility and made him a major character—hero and villain both—in the tremendously dramatic pageant of Dodger-Giant baseball.*

One of the young boys who Maglie did not frighten was a rabid Brooklyn Dodger fan named Ron Healey, who shared this story:

> *In the summer of 1951, I was walking along Bedford Avenue in back of Ebbets Field, home of the Brooklyn Dodgers. Behind the right field fence, I noticed an open window, which normally, was always closed. Little did I know, it led to the bathroom of the visiting team. That night, the Dodgers were playing the hated New York Giants. Looking out the bathroom window was Sal "the Barber" Maglie and third baseman Hank Thompson. When*

I first looked at Sal, I said, "Hi Sal," he said "Hi kid." I then said, "Hey Sal, would you sign an autograph for me?" He replied, "Sure." I realized then that there was a criss-cross, heavy duty iron screen over the window. All I had with me was my small, spiral notebook I used for homework and a short pencil. I asked Sal, "How can I give you this notebook?" He replied, "Just pull a sheet of paper out, take the pencil, roll the pencil inside the paper, and pass it through the screen." So, I tore out a piece of paper, rolled the pencil inside the paper, and passed it through the screen. Sal and Hank both signed it for me and passed it back. From that day forward, even though I was a big Dodgers fan, I always liked Sal Maglie as a person. While I was in the US Navy in 1956, Maglie was traded to the Dodgers and pitched a no hitter. I was very happy for him.

Like Maglie, Arthur C. Vance—or "Dazzy," as he's best known—didn't get his act together until he was over thirty. But when he finally got his chance to stick, he dominated.

So much so, he ultimately was an easy pick to fill out our Legends staff.

Baseball author and founder of the award-winning Seamheads.com, Mike Lynch, was one of the folks we consulted during the selection process. When I informed him about the selection of Vance as the Legends' fifth starter, he concurred. "I'm a big Dazzy Vance fan and would choose him for a handful of reasons," said Lynch. "You already have a Met, Yankee and two Giants, so it would be nice to see a Dodger on your staff. In fact, you could write that to justify his inclusion, if necessary."

I told Lynch that I didn't know about his fandom of Vance, but I was encouraged by his reply.

First off, Lynch is a sabermetric guy, so while he might say he's a fan of a player, his analysis was going to be evidence-based.

After looking at your rotation, I think you nailed it....I respect Marty [Appel] and if you want to throw Ruffing out there every five days to get his bat in the lineup I wouldn't blame you. Among HOF starting pitchers, he has the most offensive WAR and among all modern day starters, he's second only to Smoky Joe Wood. But on the mound, he just doesn't stack up. I checked WAR, WAR/162 games, and Runs Saved Above Average and [Ruffing] is nowhere near the others. He has more WAR than Ford, but he played 22 years to Ford's 16 and his WAR/162 of 3.0 is lower than Ford's 3.9 and much lower than the others'. The five you chose are all in the top 50 in Runs Saved Above Average with Seaver (7), Matty

(8), and Hubbell (10) in the top 10, and Ford at 17. Vance is at 43 but
Ruffing is at 95 tied with Corey Kluber.

Vance's remarkable story starts in 1912 as a twenty-one-year-old fireballer who lacked control. But as they say, you can't teach speed, and by the spring of 1915, he was a Pittsburgh Pirate. He promptly lost his major-league debut on April 16 and was immediately traded to the New York Yankees, where he lost all of his three decisions.

It was back to the minors for three more years, where his control problem would resurface. But he managed to get another major-league trial in 1918 with the Yanks, which was disastrous.

Two more years of minor-league stumbles and a sore arm landed Dazzy in New Orleans in 1920. There, thanks to a lousy poker hand, his life was changed forever.

On his *Joe Blogs* site, author Joe Posnanski tells a story I learned about for the first time when I started writing this book:

> *In 1920, he played in the most famous poker game in baseball history. It happened in New Orleans. Vance was 29 years old, he had exactly zero victories in the big leagues, and he couldn't pitch because of arm problems that nobody could quite figure out. During the game, Vance apparently lost a heartbreaking hand, and he smashed his arm on the table. The pain was so intense that he almost fell to his knees. He'd never felt THAT kind of pain before. The next day, he went to a doctor whose name, sadly, has been lost to history. The doctor did something. Bill James guesses that he removed some bone chips, but we don't really know and never will know. All we know is that after that, Dazzy Vance became one of the greatest pitchers in baseball history.*

So, the bad poker hand led to the surgery that saved his pitching arm. But it would take another lucky roll of the dice to set up one of the most unlikely success stories in the history of the game.

Now healthy, Vance started to mow down batters in New Orleans, winning twenty-one games that season. No one seemed to care, however. He was thirty-one and had pitched for a decade in the minors and had failed three times as a MLB starter. However, Dazzy's catcher, Hank DeBerry, was a sought-after prospect.

The Brooklyn Dodgers (then called the Robins) were scouting the young backstop and wanted to purchase his contract. There was a catch: the

Maybe Dazzy should have been called "Dominant" Vance instead. *Photo by The Baseball Hall of Fame.*

Pelicans wouldn't sell DeBerry to Brooklyn unless they took Dazzy along for the ride. At first, the Brooks balked, not wanting to get stuck with a thirty-one-year-old tomato can. However, DeBerry stepped up for his batterymate and insisted the Robins pull the trigger.

DeBerry became a top-flight defensive catcher and would be Vance's primary receiver from 1922 to 1928, a period in which Dazzy would lead the league in strikeouts each year. The dominance wasn't just in leading the league; he was fanning 200 batters when most of the league wasn't even whiffing 100. Also, despite pitching in a bandbox like Ebbets Field, he never allowed more than 15 home runs a season. Ruffing, on the other hand, allowed more than 15 home runs on eight occasions; Koosman, eleven times; Cone, nine times; Gooden, six times; and Maglie, nine times.

One great illustration of Dazzy's greatness appeared in a research paper called "One of Baseball's Most Dominant Pitchers, Dizzy Vance." (Yes, Fred Worth, professor of mathematics at Henderson State University, spelled it wrong.) Worth showed that, in 1922, Vance led the National League and was third in the majors with 134 strikeouts.

Despite pitching more than 100 fewer innings than AL leaders Urban Shocker and Red Faber, he was only 14 and 15 strikeouts behind the two, respectively.

The people with the most strikeouts in the major leagues from 1922 to 1928 were Dazzy Vance (1,338) and, in second, Burleigh Grimes (689). Vance had practically twice as many as the man behind him.

Yet Dazzy Vance, despite having played in New York and being voted into the Hall of Fame, is virtually unknown in the very town he starred in. In a piece for fangraphs.com titled "Dazzy Vance, the Ultimate Outlier," Tony Blengino asks: "Why hasn't Vance's name been passed down more prominently throughout the years? Partially due to the relative brevity of his career, but also to his lack of a postseason record. He never pitched in postseason play until a token appearance at age 43 on the 1934 Gashouse Gang Cardinals."

Even a casual baseball fan knows enough about the game to fill part of a volume called *Baseball Anecdotes*. Whether one thinks first of Ty Cobb's sharpening his spikes or Casey Stengel's releasing a live bird from beneath his cap or Lou Gehrig's four-homer game being overshadowed in the sports pages by John McGraw's retirement or Eddie Waitkus getting shot by a fan, so much of the game lies in its lore that the title of this book is very nearly a redundancy.

I'll leave you with this gem from Daniel Okrent and Steve Wulf's *Baseball Anecdotes*.

> *On the infamous play in which three daffy Dodger base runners wound up on third base in a 1926 game against the Boston Braves, they quote what Dazzy Vance said (according to a contemporary) while still lying on the ground after sliding back into third: "Mr. Umpire, fellow teammates, and members of the opposition. If you carefully peruse the rules of our national pastime you will find that there is one and only one protagonist in rightful occupancy of this hassock—namely yours truly, Arthur C. Vance.'*

Now, that is what you call a legend.

II

MIKE PIAZZA

Mike Piazza legitimized the Mets immediately at a time when the Yankees had center stage in New York. It was cool. We didn't have a lot of big name guys on that team. But when Mike got there, we had our rock star.
—*Al Leiter*

I have always felt a special connection to Mike Piazza.

I was living in Hollywood when Piazza made his major-league debut with the Los Angeles Dodgers on September 1, 1992. Back then, I was an actor trying to find my way. If it weren't for ramen noodles and baseball, I'd have gone nuts.

I watched a lot of Dodger and Angel games that year (bad baseball: the Dodgers went 63-99 and the Angels 70-92). I remember reading about Piazza's debut for the Dodgers, and I immediately liked him. He didn't light the world on fire in his first twenty-one games (.232./.284/.319), but I did happen to watch the game when he hit his first career home run, a three-run shot off of San Francisco Giant reliever Steve Reed on September 12, 1992.

I didn't know it then, but Mike Piazza would become one of the best players to ever wear a Met uniform and cement his place as the best hitting catcher of all time.

Before I continue, you might be wondering at this point why Mike Piazza is the Gotham Baseball Legends catcher.

It wasn't an easy decision.

The catchers on the Gotham Baseball ballot were all Hall of Famers: the Yankees' Yogi Berra and Brooklyn's Roy Campanella each won three MVP awards, and Giant backstop Roger Bresnahan was Christy Mathewson's catcher and the first backstop in to be enshrined in Cooperstown. Piazza wasn't even the Mets' entry on the ballot, as I put Gary Carter on it. (I'll explain later.)

When he saw the ballot, Marty Appel asked, "Where's Bill Dickey?" Another proponent of Dickey was John Pennisi, who told me years ago that if I ever wrote a book about the best New York catcher of all time, and it wasn't Dickey, he wouldn't do the artwork. (Ha! He did it anyway. Isn't it amazing?)

First off, unlike Dickey (Ruth, Gehrig), Berra (DiMaggio, Mantle) and Campanella (Robinson, Hodges, Snider), Piazza never had a Hall of Fame–caliber teammate to protect his spot in the lineup. I'm not trying to diminish what those other players accomplished, just pointing out that during Piazza's Met career, he was always the No. 1 guy.

He was also a better hitter than all of them. "Mike Piazza is the best right-handed hitter I have ever seen, forget about best-hitting catcher," *New York Post* columnist Mike Vaccaro told me when I interviewed him for this book.

"Piazza is far-and-away the best hitting catcher the modern game has ever seen, especially when compared to his Hall of Fame brethren," wrote Steven Martano of beyondtheboxscore.com. "He finished his career with a 142 OPS+ and leaves all other catchers, both in the Hall and out, in the dust as far as home runs. His 427 dingers are nearly 40 more than Johnny Bench (who played a full season more than Piazza) and 50 more than Carlton Fisk (who played 500 more games!)."

The popular narrative is that Piazza was an all-hit, no-field catcher. Was he any good at throwing out runners? Nope. But he was really good at everything else.

"With Piazza behind the plate, pitchers allowed an OPS 25 points lower, and an unintentional walk rate 10 percent lower than they did while throwing to different catchers in the same seasons," illustrated Dan Fox for FiveThirtyEight.com.

Mark Simon, for ESPN.com, noted that former Dodger batterymate Ismael Valdez can vouch for Piazza's work. He pitched twelve years in the majors but had his best seasons from 1994 to 1997, when he threw to Piazza. His strikeout-to-walk rate was 3.1:1 when Piazza caught him, 1.9:1 when others did.

"He was athletic, a strong guy, and a workaholic," Valdez said. "He said, 'If you want me to move outside, inside, whatever, I will do whatever it takes for you to have success.' And he did."

Simon interviewed Piazza's manager when he was with the Mets, Bobby Valentine, who believed that Piazza's success as a pitch framer and pitch blocker was the product of two things: physical strength and pitching recognition.

"His hands were really strong," Valentine said. "We had a couple of guys whose pitches tended to take the glove out of the strike zone—Al Leiter with his slider/cutter and Armando Benitez with his forkball. Mike was able to not only keep his glove in the zone, but he could bring the ball back. [With Benitez] he was able to keep the ball up when it was breaking down at 92 to 93 miles per hour."

So why was Gary Carter the entry on the ballot for the Mets, and not Piazza?

Much like the decision to place Roy White over Dave Winfield in left field for the Yankees, I made the call and hoped the voters would decide. Frankly—and I am not ashamed to admit this—I loved Gary Carter, and not just because he helped the Mets win the 1986 World Series.

It was personal. Carter touched many lives during his career, including my own.

In the summer of 1986, it became apparent that my sister Nicole would need a kidney transplant. My dad—a huge Gary Carter fan dating back to his Expos days—was the donor, and when the Mets were taking on the Astros in the NLCS, we spent most of that postseason watching the games on hospital TVs. After the World Series, in which Carter did more than his share, my father wrote a letter to Gary telling him about our family. Not long after, both my dad and my sister received autographed pictures of Carter with personal messages attached, as well as an invitation for my dad, mom and sister to meet Gary at Shea Stadium. They did so during the 1987 season, and my family could not have been more touched by the personal way the All-Star catcher spoke with my sister.

Gary Carter was the missing piece for the 1986 Mets. *Photo by The Baseball Hall of Fame.*

I caught up with Gary in 2001, when I was covering the first season of the Brooklyn Cyclones. Carter had spent a few seasons with the Mets as a roving catching instructor and was in Brooklyn that week working with the Cyclones catchers. After interviewing him for a piece I was preparing about Brett Kay, the young Cyclones catcher, he and I had a few minutes to chat. In what turned into an almost forty-five-minute conversation, I explained who I was and thanked him for his kindness to my family. Instead of saying, "Oh, I remember" or some other phony platitude, he simply asked how my dad and sister were doing. (My sister had just received a second transplant, this time from my brother.) When I told him that my dad was great and my sister was doing even better, he grabbed me by the shoulders. "That is amazing," Carter said. "God bless your family, and God bless your sister."

So sue me, I loved "The Kid."

In any event, I had made it clear that no matter who was on the ballot, I would take the voters' final decision into consideration.

"This ballot will probably be split along fan loyalty lines, but we have been surprised by this type of voting before," I wrote on the original ballot that was distributed to fans. "In any event, we've allowed each ballot to have a write-in option, so if we've omitted any candidate for any spot, feel free to vote along those lines."

One poster wrote, "[It's] ridiculous not to include Piazza, who had more great years in NY than Gary Carter, and is only the most dominant hitter of all time at his position. Gary Carter would be Piazza's backup on any all-time Mets team. I think a lot of folks agree—I bet most of the write-in votes are for Piazza, and write-ins are winning."

He was right. Piazza (46 percent) beat out Berra (26 percent) and Carter (18 percent) by virtue of the write-in ballot. I was shocked by the result. I really didn't think anyone was going to beat out Berra, given his love affair with both the Mets and Yankee fanbases.

The Dodgers drafted Piazza in the sixty-second round (1,390th overall) in 1988 as a favor to manager Tommy Lasorda, who was a childhood friend of Vince Piazza, Mike's dad. The twelve-year-old who received batting tips from the immortal Ted Williams would win the National League Rookie of the Year Award in 1993.

He'd spend the next several years crushing the baseball as the king of the West Coast glamour boys. In seven years as a Dodger, he hit 177 homers, drove in 563 runs and posted a .331 batting average. But on June 23, 1996, Tommy Lasorda stepped down as Dodger manager. Six months later, Peter O'Malley told everyone he was selling the team.

The high bidder was Rupert Murdoch's Fox Group, and suddenly, Mike Piazza—born to be a Dodger—was now what was wrong with the franchise?

In 1997, Piazza had his best season ever, hitting .362 with 40 homers and 124 RBIs, and he spent the offseason and spring training of 1998 trying to work out a new contract with the new ownership group. Piazza wanted a seven-year extension that would have made him baseball's first $100 million man. The Dodgers offered a six-year, $81 million contract, and Piazza turned it down.

Piazza was determined to have an even better year in 1998, and he figured that if he led the team to a World Series, he'd get his deal and become a Dodger for life.

However, things didn't turn out quite that way. The Fox suits didn't want to take a chance that they would lose Piazza as a free agent, so they traded away their best and most popular player.

The Dodger fanbase would lament; Met fans would rejoice.

I first heard about the much-anticipated trade of Piazza to the Mets while riding the Q27 bus to my mom and dad's house. I had been listening to WFAN radio for days, hoping beyond hope that my Mets would get the hitter they so desperately needed.

"The Mets got Piazza!" I yelled as I walked in the door. Even my mom was excited.

It was a great time to be a Met fan. Manager Bobby Valentine finally had the impact bat he'd been begging ownership for. Adding the power-hitting All-Star to the lineup could be the final piece to a World Series title.

It didn't hurt that he was an Italian American playing for a team in a city that was full of Italian Americans.

A few days earlier, it seemed unlikely. I had been at the Mets Clubhouse store in Manhattan, and the mood among Met fans there was that the Cubs would deal for Piazza because of statements made by general manager Steve Phillips. "We already have an All-Star catcher," Phillips told Mike Francesa and Chris "Mad Dog" Russo, the hosts of WFAN's *Mike & the Mad Dog*. He was of course referring to Todd Hundley, who had hit 41 home runs two years earlier but was on the disabled list with a bad elbow.

I liked Hundley as a player. He wore number 9, my good-luck number, and he was a ray of light in the terrible season of 1996, when he hit 41 home runs to break Roy Campanella's record of 40 as a catcher. He was a solid two-way player.

But he was no Mike Piazza.

Mike Piazza made Shea Stadium rock again. *Photo by Bill Menzel.*

The newspapers and radio stations were screaming for the Mets to make the deal.

The Mets' co-owners, Nelson Doubleday and Fred Wilpon, were split on Piazza. "I thought Mr. Piazza was a viable man for the New York Mets and a viable man for New York City and one hell of a star and we ought to take a shot at him," Doubleday told the *New York Times*' Murray Chass.

Fred Wilpon was of another mind.

Part of Wilpon's reluctance was that Piazza had rebuffed the Dodgers' six-year, $81 million offer earlier in the season, which prompted the trade to the Marlins. Wilpon didn't want to get into a bidding war, but he praised the deal after it was made and actually took credit after the fact for making it happen.

But according to the *New York Observer*, Wilpon may have showed his hand as to where his feelings actually lay: "Mr. Wilpon invited Mr. Hundley to his home in Glen Cove, L.I., and gave him his 1986 World Series ring. The gesture said a lot—said more, really, than Mr. Wilpon's subsequent attempts to claim partial credit for the Piazza trade in the press."

Piazza hit an RBI double in his first game as a Met, creating a buzz that hadn't been seen in quite some time at Shea Stadium. It didn't last. The team started to lose games, and despite Piazza's productivity—by far the best of anyone on the team—it seemed as if the crowds in Flushing were blaming Mike for the team's missing the postseason, punctuated by a season-ending five-game losing streak.

Now, he hit .348 with 23 home runs and 76 RBIs in 103 games for the Mets, including batting .347/.414/.663 in August and .378/.457/.720 in September, but the reaction to Piazza was strange, even for New York standards.

I mean, people were booing Mike like he owed them money.

Maybe it was because no one was sure if Piazza was staying; maybe it's because fans wanted to see if he was built for the New York spotlight.

Fred Wilpon's strange interview with the *New York Times* on August 29 certainly didn't help.

> "I hope Mike wants to stay, but I don't know," Wilpon said. "It's hard to get a feel. I don't think he's saying anything to anyone."
>
> When Wilpon was asked if he feels the booing Piazza has endured at home will have a bearing on the Mets' efforts to re-sign him, Wilpon said, "Without question, yes."
>
> "The issue is," Wilpon went on, "I think he's played hard. At times, he's played very well. At other times, he's played O.K. But the fact is that the booing has affected him. How could it not affect someone?"

Wilpon's reluctance to embrace the idea of signing Piazza for the long term was likely as strong as his affinity for Hundley. Add to the mix that the media covering the team loved Hundley, disliked Valentine and didn't yet trust Piazza, and many fans got mixed messages about the team and were at a loss.

I wasn't sure what Piazza would do myself, but my feeling was that anyone booing Piazza was an idiot. I also surmised that while Piazza wasn't used to the tough love of the Shea Stadium crowd, about every single inning of every big-league game of his career had been on the big stage. So, if he was truly great, I thought to myself back then, he'll want to play in the biggest town there is.

I guessed right.

"I had no idea, I would end up with the Mets when the 1998 season started," Piazza told *Sports Collectors Digest*. "For me, it was a tough time in New York at first. I wasn't playing well by any means. Then I just decided to do the best I could….Sometimes in life, change is difficult and it's tough. It knocks you out of your comfort zone. Sometimes, you just have to go along for the ride and make the best of it and good things happen."

The worst thing the Mets did was fail to build a better team around Piazza.

Piazza spent eight years with the Mets and helped take them to the postseason in 1999 and then all the way to the World Series the following season. Piazza was a seven-time All-Star with the Mets and set a team record with 124 RBI and hit 40 home runs in 1999 and then finished with 38 home runs and drove in 113 runs in 2000.

In 2001, the team was just 82-80 and finished under .500 in 2002, 2003 and 2004.

I interviewed Piazza as he approached the home-run record for catchers in 2004. We sat in the Met dugout at Shea Stadium and talked about the record, but as that had been in the tabloids for weeks, I thought other aspects of his career would be just as important.

Knowing Mike was a fan of baseball history and proud of his Italian American heritage, I asked him about what he and his dad, Vince, had talked about when he passed Joe DiMaggio on the home-run list. "That was pretty unreal," he said. "My dad was proud."

Piazza hit 427 career home runs; the great Joe DiMaggio had 361 with nearly the same amount of at-bats. Though honored by the comparison, Piazza modestly declines to accept it as anything but statistical curiosity. "Obviously, I know how much Joe DiMaggio means to the game of baseball," Piazza said. "My dad watched him play when he was growing up, so there's a strong connection there. Hey, I enjoyed the moment, but it's really not in me to dwell on things like that. The game itself is what drives me. Getting better every day, that's the kind of thing I like to focus on."

I also noted that Piazza played the majority of his games in Dodgers Stadium and Shea Stadium, hardly hitter's parks.

"I'm proud of that," he laughed. "Not too many people ever bring that up."

Like DiMaggio, who lost more than his share of home runs to old Yankee Stadium's Death Valley in left center, I asked him if he ever wondered what kind of numbers he could have put up if he had played the majority of his games in the friendly confines of Wrigley Field.

Piazza smiled. "I've never looked at where I've played as an obstacle, it's something I've done my whole career," said Piazza. "[You] take what could be a negative and turn it into a positive. Had I played somewhere else, sure, I may have had some better power numbers. But I don't think it would feel as satisfying. That's how I like to look at it."

In 2005, his last season in New York, he hit 19 home runs, drove in 62 and slashed .251/.326/.452.

Despite the big-splash signings of Pedro Martinez and Carlos Beltran, the team finished at just 83-79.

Gotham Baseball's Aaron Ross covered Piazza's return to Shea Stadium as a San Diego Padre in 2006 in a story titled "One More Piazza Party."

The hulking figure garbed in the tools of ignorance walked from the bullpen out onto the familiar field of Shea Stadium and into the comforting applause of thousands of fans, like he'd done hundreds of times before in the past. But this time was different. This time, he emerged from the opponent's bullpen with a peculiar #33 sewn on the back of his blue San Diego Padres road jersey. He was a visitor, yet still he was welcomed home.

Mike Piazza's return to Flushing on Aug. 8, the scene from which eight years of his baseball life took place, was no ordinary homecoming. Under the ever-watchful surveillance of the New York media and the adoring eyes of a near sold-out audience, Piazza received a gift from the baseball gods that normally eludes those without championships…a hero's welcome and the heartfelt thanks from the New York fans.

"(It was) Awesome, from start to finish," Piazza said. "I totally didn't think it was going to be this much support. I thought it would be nice, but I was overwhelmed, from the start of batting practice to the end of the game. It was awesome."

Piazza bids farewell to New York. He's now in the Hall of Fame as a Met. *Photo by Bill Menzel.*

If this August marked his final in-game appearance at Shea Stadium, then he gave his faithful fans one last set of magical moments that only Mike Piazza could deliver.

Piazza wound up going 1-4 that night, while his Padres went on to lose the game to the Mets, 3–2. The next day, he hit two home runs and got a standing ovation each time. He would end his career in Oakland in 2007.

On January 6, 2016, it was announced that Mike Piazza would be going into Cooperstown, and with a Mets cap. I had a feeling he would get in that year and, fittingly, found out about his induction at a local batting cage. There was a large television mounted on the wall, and I was watching my phone and the TV screen as it got closer to 6:00 p.m. on January 6.

My son and his baseball teammates were taking part in their first winter workout, and many of the boys' parents were also on hand. We cheered the news of Piazza's induction and quickly took action. The facility has a very large poster of Derek Jeter on the wall, and a parent was quickly dispatched to the manager's office to inform him that a Piazza poster should go up on the wall somewhere soon.

Later that year, the Mets retired his uniform no. 31 in a memorable and heart-warming ceremony at Citi Field.

"How can I put into words my love, thanks and appreciation for New York Mets' fans?" Piazza said. "You have given me the greatest gift and graciously taken me into your family. This brings me back to the best time of my life. The eight years we spent together went by way too fast. Looking back into this crowd of blue and orange brings me back to the greatest time of my life. The thing I miss most is making you cheer."

I miss the way he hit home runs, and I described it once this way for *Mets Inside Pitch* magazine:

> *The fluid motion of the bat explodes through the strike zone. The sound of the ball connecting with the barrel is a dramatic thwack that causes devastation (for the pitcher) and pure joy (for the hitter) at the same instant. Then the familiar lean, the hands suspended for a moment...then, the squint. Yeah, it's gone. Finally, the graceful stroll around the bases. Mike Piazza has gone yard once again.*

Mike Piazza made Shea Stadium rock again.

He and Tom Seaver, who ceremoniously closed the doors at Shea in 2008 and opened the doors at Citi Field, are Mets batterymates in the Hall of Fame.

It doesn't get any better than that.

12

LOU GEHRIG

What visions burn, what dreams possess him,
Seeker of the night?
The faultless velvet of the diamond,
The mounting roar of 80,000 voices
And Gehrig coming to bat
—Thomas Wolfe, 1934

New York has been blessed with some of the greatest first basemen of all time.

The New York Giants had Bill Terry, who slashed 341/.393/.506 with 154 home runs, 1,078 RBI and an OPS of .899 over fourteen seasons. He was also the last National Leaguer to hit .400, reaching .401 in 1930. That year, *Baseball Magazine* called Terry "baseball's greatest first baseman."

Gil Hodges was one of the most beloved players to play in Ebbets Field when he manned first base for the hometown Brooklyn Dodgers. He was also the first National League first baseman to post seven consecutive seasons with at least 23 home runs and 100 RBI. The only other player to do that is Albert Pujols. Hodges was a great defender as well and is considered the best right-handed defensive first baseman of all time. "Gil Hodges fields better on one leg than anybody else I got on two," said Casey Stengel.

The Mets' Keith Hernandez has often been called a borderline Hall of Famer, many citing his superb defense and leadership when he joined New York in a midseason trade in 1983. After several seasons of truly bad

Met baseball from 1978 to 1983, Hernandez helped the team become one of MLB's best in the mid-1980s, winning the World Series in 1986. He slashed .297/.387/.429 with 80 home runs and 468 RBI with an OPS of .816 as a Met. But it was his defense—he was considered by some the best defensive first baseman ever—that always stood out for most. "[Hernandez] won 11-straight Gold Gloves, and probably should have a couple of more," wrote Jeff Pearlman in *The Bad Guys Won*. "He could go left or right with equal aplomb; charge balls with remarkable grace; handle throws from the worst third basemen ever (see Jefferies, Gregg). Having grown up in New York watching the '80s Mets, I can't recall Hernandez ever not scooping out a ball. He was, simply, remarkable. Unparalleled. Magical."

That is quite a cast (and quite a ballot), but both the voters and I say that Lou Gehrig is simply the best first baseman in New York baseball history.

I'm a lifelong Met fan, but Gehrig was always one of my favorites, historically. For starters, *Pride of the Yankees* was watched at my house whenever it was on, and even that audience of Yankee haters sobbed the hundreds of times we watched it. I admit that, as a young boy, I instantly fell in love with Teresa Wright, the actress who played Eleanor Gehrig. She was in Marlon Brando's first film, *The Men*, and in the masterpiece *The Best Years of Our Lives*. All the way until Francis Ford Coppola's *The Rainmaker* in 1997, the crush remained.

In praise of Richard Sandomir's book about the iconic film, *The Pride of the Yankees: Lou Gehrig, Gary Cooper, and the Making of a Classic*, Marty Appel wrote, "To this day, we see Pride of the Yankees as an accurate portrayal of Lou Gehrig."

Playing Gehrig in *Pride of the Yankees* is arguably Cooper's most famous role. He was nominated for an Academy Award but lost the Oscar to James Cagney for his role as George M. Cohan in *Yankee Doodle Dandy*.

Those damn Yankees will get you every time.

Gehrig was a native New Yorker, a city kid born and raised in the Yorkville section of Manhattan. He was a star high school athlete, excelling at both football and baseball at Commerce High, and was recognized by both the *Chicago Tribune* and the *New York Daily News* as a young man with a ton of potential.

Shortly after Lou enrolled at Columbia University, the New York Giants arranged for him to have a tryout at the Polo Grounds. He put on a hitting display that made everyone, especially manager John McGraw, take notice. But then he took the field.

According to Gehrig's SABR biographer James Lincoln Ray, Gehrig let the first grounder hit his way roll through his legs. "Get this fellow out of here!" McGraw told his coaches. "I've got enough lousy players without another one showing up."

That's how close Mugsy got to having Ruth (see chapter 5) and Gehrig on his Giants instead of the Yankees, whom he loathed.

Gehrig instead focused on playing ball at Columbia University, where he caught the notice of Yankee superscout Paul Krichell. SABR's Ray writes:

> *On April 26, 1923, a Yankees scout named Paul Krichell took a train from New York City to New Brunswick, New Jersey, to watch a game between Columbia and Rutgers. While on the train, Columbia's baseball coach, Andy Coakley, struck up a conversation with Krichell and told him about Gehrig, advertising the sophomore as a pitcher who was "also a good hitter." Gehrig hit two home runs in three at-bats against Rutgers, and Krichell was so impressed that he telephoned Yankees general manager Ed Barrow and told him that he had just discovered another Babe Ruth.*

It wasn't the first or last time Gehrig would be compared to the Babe, but maybe Appel puts it best in *Pinstripe Empire: The New York Yankees from Before the Babe to After the Boss*, describing Gehrig as "Ruth without drama, Ruth without nightlife, Ruth without scandal."

The narrative about Gehrig has often been that he played in Ruth's shadow and, of course, had the premature end to his career because of amyotrophic lateral sclerosis (ALS). Not enough time is spent on just how great his playing career was. I say that he made Ruth a better player. I believe that Gehrig's consistent greatness made Ruth realize that he had a partner in offensive crime against the rest of baseball's pitchers.

For two years, the future "Iron Horse" was relegated to crushing the ball in the Yankees' Hartford farm club. Because of the presence of slick-fielding and clutch-hitting first baseman Wally Pipp, who averaged .306/.361/.437 and 104 RBI from 1921 to 1924, Gehrig played in only twenty-three big-league games between 1923 and 1924. It wasn't until 1925 that Gehrig was given an opportunity to play every day.

The legend is that Pipp had a headache and it cost him his job. What actually happened was that, coming off a 1924 season in which the Yankees had finished in second place, the 1925 squad was slumping to start the season, including Pipp. On Tuesday, June 2, 1925, the struggling Yankees were just a half-game ahead of the last-place Boston Red Sox. So, Yankee manager Miller Huggins sent his rookie to first base instead of Wally Pipp, who was in a 13-for-79 (.165) slump.

Gehrig had three hits in an 8–5 win over the Senators, and after the game, Huggins told the *New York Evening Post*: "I was well pleased, of course, the way the youngsters hustled in there and hit like regulars....But I can't say yet that the change is a permanent one. I think it'll pep up the team and probably get us off to a right start. After a rest the regulars may get back and we'll step right out of the slump."

Except Gehrig had different ideas, and Pipp's Yankee career was now over.

A thirty-year-old Ruth, who had reported to spring training in 1925 about thirty pounds overweight, didn't slow down when he reported for camp. The result was "The Bellyache Heard 'Round the World," which in actuality was an intestinal abscess that would keep him in a hospital bed for over a month. He'd make his season debut on June 1, a day before Gehrig's first game.

While Ruth would spend the rest of the season fighting with his manager, Gehrig was impressing Huggins. He was also making friends on the team, with the fans and in the press box.

The superstar now had an everyman sharing the same clubhouse. The big lug who forgot everyone's name now had an Atlas who kept to himself, worked hard and, even as a rookie, earned the respect of everyone around him.

Maybe that's why, in 1926, Ruth played the rest of his career as a man possessed. From 1926 to 1934, Ruth averaged a slash line of .342/.475/.688 with an OPS of 1.163.

Enough about Ruth. (See, even I'm doing it!)

In his seventeen seasons with the Yankees, of which only fourteen were full seasons, Gehrig slashed .340/.447/.632 with 493 home runs and 1,995 RBIs. He drove in more than 170 runs three times, including 185 in 1931 and *averaged* 40 doubles a season. His career OPS is 1.080, trailing only Ruth and Ted Williams for the best of all time.

Yet, as I mentioned before, when most people talk about Gehrig, it's the streak and the illness and little else. In an interview I had with Jonathan Eig, the author of *Luckiest Man: The Life and Death of Lou Gehrig*, I asked him how hard it was to avoid writing another book that missed out on highlighting Gehrig's greatness as a ballplayer. "It was hard to get that balance because starting out, the part that intrigued me most was the illness…but I realized that was a mistake," said Eig. "You had to see him on the field, you had to see him interacting with his teammates, you had to get to know the guy in the prime of his life and see what a phenomenal ballplayer he was to really care....Three quarters of the book is baseball."

So many of Gehrig's career accomplishments are lost. He was a pretty great baserunner, and what he lacked in the stolen-base department he made up for with hustle and muscle. He hit 20 triples in 1926 and compiled 10 or more triples in eight different seasons. Did you know that Gehrig stole home 15 times in his career? That puts him in the top twenty of all time. I mean, Jackie Robinson did it 19 times.

Let's talk about his fielding for a moment. Earlier in the chapter, we discussed how John McGraw threw him out of the Polo Grounds after trying to watch him field. By many accounts, he was a poor fielder early on. He committed double-digit errors in ten of his fourteen full-time seasons. But errors don't tell the whole story—neither does fielding percentage (though Gehrig's career .991 mark is pretty solid).

Many scoff at anecdotal evidence as anything but, but longtime sportswriter, author and storyteller Paul Gallico probably captured it better than any algorithm can. "There is no greater inspiration to any American boy than Lou Gehrig. For if this awkward, inept and downright clumsy player that I knew in the beginning could through sheer drive and determination turn himself into the finest first-base-covering machine in all of baseball, then nothing is impossible to any man or boy in the country."

On PinstripeAlley.com, Logan Goldberg wrote: "From 1930 to 1932, Gehrig drove in 509 runs, the most ever in a three-year span by a ridiculous margin and a feat Ruth never approached. Gehrig's 184 RBI in 1931 remain an American League record, whereas Ruth's 60 home run mark has been eclipsed seven times."

He didn't just drive them in, he also scored runs—and that was while hitting behind Ruth. In 1927, Gehrig scored 149 runs; in 1931, he scored 163 runs; and in 1936, he scored 167 runs. Only in his last full season, 1938, did he score less than 120 runs, and he still scored 115 times.

The 1938 season would be Gehrig's last full season, and if you look at his numbers in a vacuum—.295/.410/.523 with a .932 OPS, 29 home runs and 114 RBIs—you might be like, "Wow, great season for a thirty-five-year-old playing every single day."

But this was Lou Gehrig, who the year before had hit .351/.473/.643 with a 1.116 OPS, 37 HRs and 158 RBIs. His 29 homers were his lowest since 1928, and his 114 RBIs were the lowest since 1926. For forty-one games, he batted fourth and hit just .220, so manager Joe McCarthy put him in the fifth spot, and he responded by hitting .312 the rest of the way. "But then by the time you get that first hint that something's wrong in spring training and 1938, when he starts showing the first tiny little

The best first baseman in New York baseball history, Lou Gehrig. *Photo by The Baseball Hall of Fame.*

symptoms, and, you know, he goes ahead and plays another year, without even knowing anything's wrong," said Eig.

The Yankees swept the Cubs in the 1938 World Series, but Gehrig had just four singles in fourteen at-bats and didn't knock in a single run. He felt worse as the fall and winter progressed, but thinking that his stiffness was merely the routine process aging ballplayers go through, he simply told himself that in the spring, he'd work harder than everyone else and get his groove back.

However, he was terrible during spring training, and even McCarthy, who adored Gehrig, told Joe Williams of the *New York World Telegram* that he wasn't sure about his captain. "He has lost his speed, and at his age this is something he will never get back. What we don't know is whether he has lost his wrist action at the plate. If he has lost that, then we have no alternative but to get somebody else to play first base."

Most of the writers covering spring training that year were respectful of Gehrig's woes; most thought that they were simply witnessing the end of a great career, not a death sentence. As he continued to struggle, however, not everyone was so willing to give him a pass.

If McCarthy can be this worried, *Orlando Sentinel* reporter Vincent Flaherty must have thought to himself, wow, maybe this is it for Gehrig. So, according to author Ray Robinson in his book *Iron Horse*, Flaherty approached the first baseman and asked him just that. Uncharacteristically, Gehrig yelled at the writer to leave him alone. Flaherty got his revenge the next day. First, Flaherty went after the New York sportswriters, criticizing their "maudlin slobbering" over the Yankee captain.

"I am not in St. Petersburg to praise Gehrig, but rather to bury the bloke," wrote Flaherty. "When Gehrig goes, I'll be sitting in on the requiem of a selfish, surly tightwad, who milked the game of all he could and who walked through his career filled with the self-sufficient philosophy that the world owed him everything."

Wow, what a dick.

Figure more than a few Yankees (and New York writers) would have liked to put that guy through a wall. But the columnists didn't go into the locker rooms in those days, instead using their poison pens to smear players from afar.

Players like Bill Dickey were probably more worried about their friend and teammate. For the first eight games of the 1939 season, Gehrig looked as bad as he had in spring training.

Flaherty probably was patting himself on the back, and Gerig hit just .143 in his first 28 at-bats. The streak would come to an end on May 2. Gehrig had enough and pulled himself out of the lineup. He was replaced by Babe Dahlgren, who recalled: "I remember Lou taking the lineup card up to the plate that day. When he came back to the dugout he went over to the water fountain and took a drink. He started to cry. Lou stood there with a towel on his head, taking the longest drink I've ever seen anybody take."

Dahlgren was a wonderful fielder and fine hitter whose life should be a movie. I don't have the space to explain, but his grandson Matt Dahlgren wrote a great book, *Rumor in Town*, which every baseball fan should read.

The Yankees beat the Tigers that day, 22–2, and would win twenty-eight of their next thirty-two games.

Over the next several weeks, Gehrig dutifully brought the lineup to the umpires before every game and even traveled with the team. On June 12, Gehrig played in an exhibition game at Kansas City, the Yankees' top farm club. It would the last baseball game he ever played in. He grounded out in his only at-bat and made two errors in the field.

The next day, he entered the Mayo Clinic. It was there that Gehrig was diagnosed with amyotrophic lateral sclerosis (ALS), largely in part because the doctor who met with him had experienced his own mother dying of the same disease years before. The doctors also told his wife that her husband would likely not live more than two more years.

The Yankees and Gehrig told the team of his diagnosis and immediate retirement on June 21. "I knew there was something seriously wrong with him. I didn't know what it was, but I knew it was serious," said Dickey after learning about Gehrig's diagnosis. "We were in the room one day a few weeks ago, and Lou stumbled as he walked across the floor. I was reading a paper and looked up to see what he had stumbled over, but there was nothing there. I was going to ask him what had happened, but he had a strange look on his face and I didn't say anything."

Plans were made for the July 4 "Lou Gehrig Day," at which the Iron Horse gave his "Luckiest Man" speech. The ceremony would be held between games of a doubleheader.

Inexplicably, United Press International's John Cuddy, a legendary boxing writer for thirty years until his death in 1975, had a big problem with the plan to honor Gehrig on July 4. In fact, his column on the event, published on July 3, 1939, was abhorrent.

There's only one thing I see wrong about the celebration of Fourth of July, and that's the national shedding of tears about a husky named Lou Gehrig—the whole business seems goofy and uncalled for to me. I see no reason for pulling a pall over a holiday when everyone should be having a lot of fun and peanuts, popcorn, crackerjack and hotdogs....I've forgotten exactly what they said was wrong with Gehrig. Oh, yes! I do recall that the first hospital report indicated infantile paralysis of a very vague breed. But later the experts explained it wasn't infantile paralysis at all. It was something else. The ailment had one of those high-falutin' names that only people with plenty of dough or prestige can have. Personally, I don't care what Gehrig has got. But I'd like to exchange my body for his during the next 40 or 50 years, let us say. And I'm pretty sure I'd do all right regardless of the experts' argument over the Latin or Greek declensions of what Laruping Lou may or may not have.

No one really knew what was wrong with Gehrig at the time, especially the press, but Cuddy knew that when Gehrig died on June 3, 1941, his rant had proved incredibly wrong. However, no one has ever been able to find Cuddy's apology.

On November 1, 2017, Ray Robinson, a prolific baseball author and longtime newspaper and magazine editor, passed away at the age of ninety-six. When I heard of his passing, I recalled the interview I did with him at Mickey Mantle's Restaurant in 2009. During our conversation, we discussed his book *Iron Horse: Lou Gehrig in His Time*, published in 1990. Along with Eig's book, Robinson's biography focused on Gehrig as a human being instead of the mythical hero.

Appel, who arranged the interview, mentioned that Robinson wasn't just a Gehrig biographer, he was also a primary source. "Ray was at Lou Gehrig Appreciation Day in 1939," Appel said. "So you're probably not going to meet too many people that were around that day."

"I sat in the right field bleachers, 50 cents," recalled Robinson. "I was nineteen years old. And I decided at the last minute to go to the game. And I asked a friend of mine, Warren Cowan—who became a great Hollywood press agent—did he want to go with me. And he said, 'I don't think he's dying, that I think he is sick and will never play baseball again.' I think that reflected what many of those 60,000 people that were at the game felt. I don't think most of them thought he was dying. I [just] thought his baseball career was at an end."

At a time when America was in the grips of the Depression, Lou Gehrig was a son of immigrants, who came to play every day and whose determination to be great came true through hard work.

Remember the courage in the face of a death sentence, remember the streak, but never forget how truly great he was.

13

JACKIE ROBINSON

Jackie Robinson burned with a dark fire. He wanted passionately to win. He bore the burden of a pioneer and the weight made him stronger. If one can be certain of anything in baseball, it is that we shall not look upon his like again.
—*Roger Kahn*

There's no question that Jackie Robinson was a brilliant player. His numbers speak for themselves. But could he have been better?

Being black wasn't Robinson's only obstacle when he entered Major League Baseball in 1947. Sure, it was a huge factor, but consider this: he was already twenty-eight and had played just part of a season with the Kansas City Monarchs of the Negro Leagues and one season of minor-league baseball in Montreal. Then he was told he would play his rookie year at a position he'd never played in his life.

Jackie had played shortstop in 1945 with the Monarchs and second base with the Triple-A Royals in 1946. It is likely that Robinson's elite athletic ability—he was the first man to ever letter in football, track, basketball and baseball at UCLA—helped him adjust. Too many folks talk about the racism Jackie faced without acknowledging these other factors, which make his Rookie of the Year performance in 1947 all the more remarkable.

But maybe his journey could have been easier.

In my mind, I've always wondered what would have happened had Leo Durocher been Robinson's manager that first season?

I asked Jonathan Eig, the author of *Opening Day: The Story of Jackie Robinson's First Season*, if he thought Durocher would have made that first season easier for the first black MLB baseball player. "I don't think there's any doubt about it," he said. "I mean, first of all, in spring training that year, Durocher made it very clear to the Dodgers that he was not going to take any crap from anybody about Jackie. And, you know, he called out some of these players and told them right off the bat in his usual incredibly crude language, that anybody who didn't want to play with this guy because of his color to take a hike."

Baseball historian Paul Dickson, who wrote *Leo Durocher: Baseball's Prodigal Son*, said Durocher's efforts to get his team on board with Robinson lasted all through the spring. "[Durocher] would leave the games early, and [his new wife, actress Laraine Day] would leave with him," Dickson told WBUR's Bill Littlefield.

> *And the paper's saying, "Leo's going back to the hotel for a little extra innings with his new bride," and all this stuff. And Leo was going back there to take one player at a time and convince him that he had to drop this racial attitude toward Robinson. He basically sold one player after another on why they had to do this. And why—if they didn't—they were doomed. It wasn't Robinson who was doomed.*

It was Durocher, who had been an excellent shortstop in his playing days, who suggested that Jackie play first base. He knew if Jackie played second he would be shredded by opposing baserunners trying to break up double plays. Team leader Eddie Stanky was the second baseman, and the team didn't have a regular first baseman yet (Gil Hodges was a year away), so it made sense on a number of levels.

Durocher was also impressed with Robinson's fire. "You want a guy who comes to play. [Robinson] didn't just come to play, he came to beat you," Durocher told Roger Kahn. "He came to stuff the damn bat right up your ass."

Durocher's critics were many; he had made enemies throughout baseball for his bench jockeying and his off-the-field interests: gambling; hanging around with Hollywood big shots like George Raft, who had organized crime connections; and his romance with Day.

But he knew his baseball and was no bigot. "Leo Durocher was a smart man," legendary Negro League player and manager Buck O'Neil told me in 2006. "You see, he wanted to win. He didn't care who it was, or where they were from, all as long as they could play that game."

But Durocher's long-standing feud with Larry McPhail exploded as spring training came to an end. MLB commissioner Happy Chandler sided with McPhail (who had helped him get the commissioner's job) and suspended Leo for the 1947 season.

Instead of having a skipper who would have stood up to any opposing manager, player or umpire who showed any hint of bias and demand that his own team throw at anyone who persisted, he had Burt Shotton, a Rickey confidant, who was as quiet as Leo was bombastic. "KOBS" (sportswriter Dick Young's sarcastic nickname for "Kindly Old Burt Shotton") was in the dugout—literally, because Shotton wore street clothes and was forbidden to step onto the field to confront anyone.

Wouldn't Durocher have made Jackie's like much easier? This was, after all, a man who got himself in hot water with then-commissioner Kenesaw Mountain Landis for telling the *Communist Daily Worker* he would sign black players if he had the chance. "Hell, yes!," Durocher said, "I'd sign them in a minute if I got permission from the big shots."

"Durocher was one of the toughest guys in the league, and if he said Robinson played, Robinson was going to play and if any of the other teams messed with Robinson, Durocher would have been out there in their faces," said Eig.

> *Leo was a very progressive guy. He wasn't looking to be a civil rights leader, but he just wanted to win and he was ferocious. So that's the kind of guy Jackie would have really benefited from having on his side. Instead, he gets Burt Shotton, a college librarian who didn't even wear the uniform so he couldn't come out of the dugout to fight on Jackie's behalf even if you wanted to, you know, the times that Jackie got thrown at when people spiked them. You know, you want to see your manager leading the team out of the dugout and fighting for your guy and Shotton couldn't even leave the dugout because he wouldn't wear a uniform.*

Branch Rickey was a brilliant baseball man, but why he hired Shotton to be the man to lead the Dodgers has always made little sense to me. When Rickey informed the players that Durocher would be suspended, he told them not to worry. It didn't matter who their manager was, he said, they would win.

Rickey could have hired Clay Hopper, Robinson's Triple-A manager. Though Hopper had begged Rickey not to put Jackie on the Royals, he came to admire Jackie. Under Hopper, Robinson won the International League batting championship, and the Royals won the Junior World Series.

I don't know why Rickey was okay with making a decision that would add to the challenges facing Robinson on a daily basis, especially when you consider that so much of the narrative about 1947 is false.

When I interviewed Eig, it was on the *Baseball Digest LIVE* podcast I used to host at legendary baseball bar Foley's NY on West 33rd Street in Manhattan. That day, my cohost was Jim Cerny—a superb broadcaster—and we had both read the book before the interview. We knew that Eig had debunked a lot of mythology about Robinson's first year in Brooklyn, but I wanted the audience to know what Eig had written.

"What about Pee Wee Reese putting his arm around Jackie in Cincinnati?" I asked. "Isn't there a statue of the two of them outside of MCU Park where the Brooklyn Cyclones play?"

Eig chuckled. "No, it never happened. I'm convinced of it," he said.

> *I spent a lot of time with Jackie's wife Rachel talking about this. She was trying to be polite, and not trash anybody. And she said, you know, Pee Wee was a great friend to Jackie, but not in 1947. In 1947, every single person on the Dodgers was waiting to see if he would fail. And only a few of them began to warm to Jackie and to give him a chance. After he showed that he could play, after he showed that he wasn't going anywhere. But even Pee Wee Reese waited, wanting to see if Jackie was going to drop out, or if he was going to hit .210 and get sent back to the minors. Nobody wants to be remembered as the guy who put his neck out there for the colored ballplayer. That just wasn't going to happen. So Robinson was really alone that year. And any attempt by the ballplayers to say, "Oh, yeah, Jackie was my pal. I'm the one who stood up for him." Those were things they said years and years later when it was when it was easy to do that.*

In my career, I had been lucky enough to have interviewed Duke Snider, Carl Erskine and Ralph Branca over the years, so I knew what Eig was talking about. Erskine wasn't on the team in 1947, and he said he was there when it happened. (He joined the team in 1948.) Snider said it happened when the team was playing in Boston against the Braves. Branca said, "What difference does it make? Pee Wee was our leader and he accepted Jackie. Even Dixie [Walker] got used to playing with Jackie."

Well, when in doubt, go to the primary source. In 1952, Robinson told *Sport* magazine that the event occurred in Boston in 1948 and repeated the story in his 1960 book *Wait Till Next Year: The Life Story of Jackie Robinson.*

The only thing that is 100 percent true is that there is no newspaper account of the actual event.

Eig's statements make sense when you consider what the *New York Post*'s Jimmy Cannon wrote about Robinson in 1947. Cannon wrote about what Jackie went through that first season, as chronicled by the *Post*'s George Willis.

> *Cannon also was one of the first of the mainstream writers to recognize that what Robinson was going through off the field was as challenging as anything on the field.*
>
> *"In the clubhouse Robinson is a stranger,"* [Cannon] *wrote in May 1947.*
>
> *"The Dodgers are polite and courteous with him, but it is obvious he is isolated by those with whom he plays. I have never heard remarks made against him or detected any rudeness where he was concerned. But the silence is loud and Robinson never is part of the jovial and aimless banter of the locker room.*
>
> *"He is the loneliest man I have ever seen in sports."*

The guttersnipes were relentless. Even the players on his own team resented him.

Eddie Stanky, who played second base, made it clear to Robinson how he felt about playing with him. "I want you to know something," he told Robinson on the eve of the opener. "You're on this ballclub and as far as I'm concerned that makes you one of the 25 players on my team. But before I play with you, I want you to know how I feel about it. I want you to know I don't like it. I want you to know I don't like you."

However, a few weeks later, when Phillies manager Ben Chapman and his team hurled the worst kind of racial epithets at Robinson, Stanky was driven to defend Robinson, telling the Phillies, "Not one of you has the guts of a louse." Stanky was built like Robinson—he burned to win. In Jackie, he recognized a kindred spirit.

His teammates would eventually grow more tolerant of Robinson's presence on the team, but they didn't socialize with him. That's why Eig wrote *Opening Day*. "I felt like we were beginning to hear the myths more than the truth. And I wanted to really strip back the layers of mythology that has come to surround Robinson and look at exactly what happened. And I thought by crystallizing the story into one season, you could really see his impact on America. And this book is filled with stories of people whose lives were changed in that moment—not people reflecting 60 years later."

Despite the intense scrutiny, the abuse, the weight of an entire race of people counting on him, a manager who couldn't protect him and, to a lesser extent, the position change, Robinson excelled. He slashed .287/.383/.427 and led the league with 29 stolen bases. He scored 125 runs and hit 31 doubles and, despite never playing first base in his life, he led all of the Dodger regulars in fielding percentage. His daring baserunning, baseball IQ and fearlessness in the face of players sliding with their spikes up and opposing pitchers throwing at his head convinced all but the most virulent racist that he was the goods.

The offseason of 1947–48 saw Jackie celebrated by the fans. The warning of Branch Rickey prior to the 1947 season to black community leaders—"If you parade and dine Robinson too much, you will make him fat and futile"—proved to be prophetic.

Robinson showed up to spring training in the Dominican Republic at least twenty and as much thirty pounds overweight. Durocher immediately started insulting him, calling him "fatso" in the press, believing that Jackie would be motivated by the public shaming.

Robinson, who was now twenty-nine years old, was not a player who responded to abuse, and whatever relationship the two had built beforehand quickly deteriorated. By midseason, the team was just 35-37, and Durocher was dispatched across town to the hated Giants and KOBS was back in the dugout.

In his autobiography, Robinson said his anger may have been misplaced:

> To get me in shape, Leo put me through some furious physical paces [in 1948]. They were humiliating because rookies, reporters and teammates were all onlookers. Leo also kept after me verbally, and as the world knows, he is a magnificent tongue lasher. At the time I thought he was being too excessive, but later I realized he was only doing what was necessary, and even though his comments hurt, I could not forget that Durocher had done all he could the previous year to help ease my way into the majors....I think that Leo felt I had not given him my best effort and was working harder for Shotton. That wasn't true but on the playing field Leo and I got into a number of hassles that were picked up by the press. Leo and I were alike in so many ways, and that could have been part of our problem. But no matter how many verbal insults were exchanged, I believe we never lost the respect we had for each other's abilities.

Robinson and the team responded to Shotton and finished 84-70, just missing the postseason and finishing in third place. Robinson overcame his

In 1949, Jackie Robinson hit .342 and was the National League MVP. *Photo by The Baseball Hall of Fame.*

slow start and finished with a team-high 85 RBIs, scored 108 runs, hit 38 doubles, struck out just 37 times in 574 at-bats and slashed .296/.367/.453 with an OPS of .820.

Before the start of Robinson's third season, in 1949, Rickey told Jackie, "You can be yourself now." The gloves were off.

In what would be his finest season, Robinson simply destroyed the rest of the National League. He batted .342/.432/.528 with an OPS of .960, drove in 124 RBIs, stole 37 bases and hit 38 doubles. He was voted by the fans to start at second base in the All-Star Game, and after the season, he was voted the NL's Most Valuable Player.

It was the start of a six-season period in which Robinson was as good as any player in baseball and perhaps its best all-around player. From 1949 to 1954, Jackie slashed .327/.428/.505 with a .933 OPS, averaging 16 home runs, 87 RBIs, 20 stolen bases, 81 walks and just 28 strikeouts per season.

In 1950, Walter O'Malley, tiring of Rickey's presence in the organization, forced him out. Robinson would never forgive the move. "O'Malley knew I felt deeply about Mr. Rickey, and consequently, I became a target of his insecurity," Jackie wrote in his autobiography.

O'Malley also fired Shotton and hired Chuck Dressen, whom Rachel Robinson said was Jackie's favorite manager. The presence of Dressen—who may have been even more of an egomaniac than Leo Durocher—would preside over the 1951 collapse. He would also lead the powerful pennant winners of 1952–53.

Dressen insisted on a three-year contract after the 1953 season, and O'Malley declined to change his practice of one-year contracts and hired minor-league manager Walter Alston instead. The Dodgers would finally win a World Series for Brooklyn in 1955, but Jackie wasn't quite the player he had been just a year earlier. His offense—hitting just .256/.378/.363—was the worst of his career, and he played the majority of his games at third base. In the World Series, after Robinson hit just .182 in the first six games, Alston benched him in Game 7.

In his final season, Robinson's skills deteriorated as rapidly as his relationships with O'Malley and Alston had, and at the end of the season, he knew it was time to call it a career.

As the Dodgers and the rest of baseball didn't see fit to offer Robinson any chance at a job of significance—a trade to the New York Giants had been turned down—Jackie spent the rest of his life trying to make a difference. He was estranged from baseball for much of his remaining years.

In 1962, Robinson was elected to the National Baseball Hall of Fame. In 1966, George Vescey of the *New York Times*, assigned a story on the absence of black coaches and managers in baseball, interviewed Robinson. "When I called for the prearranged interview, he turned the theme around, asking how many black journalists were in the sports department where I worked. Umm, none, I said, thereby touching off a monologue on lack of opportunity everywhere. That's what I'm talking about, he said. I consider the lecture a highlight of my career."

At the age of fifty-three, Jackie suffered a fatal heart attack at his home in Stamford, Connecticut. He died on October 24, 1972, only months after his number 42 was officially retired by the Dodgers.

Since 2004, Major League Baseball has celebrated Jackie Robinson Day, commemorating the man who broke baseball's color line once and for all. As has been a tradition each April 15, all players and on-field personnel wear Jackie's iconic number 42.

However, while everyone wearing 42 is a wonderful tribute, I've often thought there's a better way to honor Robinson. My proposal is this: Keep Robinson's number retired throughout the game, but each year, MLB should partner with the Jackie Robinson Foundation and select a player from each league to wear "42" for the upcoming season. As a Jackie Robinson Ambassador, that player—or coach, or manager—would spend the season educating people about and honoring Jackie's legacy in each city that particular team goes to.

What better way to honor a legendary player who changed so much?

14

DEREK JETER

I'm trying to think who the best Yankee shortstop I've ever seen is, and I keep coming back to this kid [Jeter].
—Phil Rizzuto

My first-ever sports assignment was covering Opening Day at Yankee Stadium in 1995.

It wasn't my first time at Yankee Stadium, but I was still amazed at the energy of the venue. It was the first game in the Bronx after the brutal 1994 work stoppage, which likely cost Yankee favorite and team captain Don Mattingly his best shot at a World Series win.

As I watched, it was obvious that this Yankees crowd loved "Donnie Baseball," and this Yankee team, after being down so long—their last postseason appearance at that point had been their losing effort in the 1981 World Series—was going to be good.

They won that day, 8–6. Mattingly went 0-for-5, and the Yankee shortstop was Tony Fernandez. It would be the last time in twenty years somebody other than Derek Jeter would be the team's shortstop on Opening Day.

Two words: Felix Fermin. That's how close the New York Yankees came to blowing its Core Four dynasty.

It was the spring of 1996, and rookie shortstop Derek Jeter wasn't wowing the brass in Tampa, and owner George Steinbrenner was very nervous.

There was a large contingent of folks that wanted Jeter to be the starting shortstop in 1996. That chorus was led by former GM and now scout

Gene Michael, who did not have his contract renewed by Steinbrenner after the Yankees had been defeated by the Mariners in the 1995 ALDS. However, despite his demotion, Michael was still the most influential voice in Yankeeland.

Steinbrenner advisor Clyde King, who, like Michael, had served in several capacities for "Big Stein" over the years, wasn't sold on Jeter, and he reportedly whispered as much in his boss's ear. Then, near the end of spring training, Fernandez fractured his elbow (out for the year). Pat Kelly was already hurt, and the only veteran middle infielder in camp was Mariano Duncan.

Convinced by King that the Yankees needed an everyday shortstop, Big Stein called an emergency meeting and told his baseball people that the Yankees needed to send Jeter back to Triple-A, and he wanted new GM Bob Watson to trade Mariano Rivera to Seattle for shortstop Felix Fermin. Fermin had a good season in 1994, hitting a career-high .317, but in 1995, he had hit just .195. Michael had nearly traded Rivera in 1995 to the Tigers for David Wells, but after seeing his young right-hander's velocity jump from ninety-one to ninety-five miles per hour, he decided not to move Rivera.

Convinced that Jeter was the once and future shortstop for the Yankees, Michael would not agree with Steinbrenner to deal away Rivera for a player of Fermin's ordinary pedigree. The room was a united front; no one was afraid of King, and they knew that Michael had a knack for getting his way with "The Boss."

It helped that new manager Joe Torre was also a Jeter fan. "I did have a sense early on that there was something special about him," Torre told *USA Today*'s Ted Berg. "He didn't have a very good spring, but he never seemed to panic. He knew how to win without going out there and doing it with his mouth but with his actions. You knew initially that there was something different about this guy."

As for Fermin, he was released in April by Seattle. The Yankees gave him a look-see in the minors for seven games in May at Triple-A Columbus, but he did little to prove that he was any kind of answer and was let go. The Cubs then picked him up. He hit .125 and in August was released and subsequently returned.

Just imagine: losing Jeter and Mariano in the same deal? For Felix Fermin?

In any event, Jeter did struggle at the start of the season, but Torre's steady hand and GM Bob Watson's steadfastness as a real buffer between his manager and Steinbrenner allowed the rookie to find his footing.

Michael knew Jeter would get better, eventually, as the kid from Kalamazoo had already showed his resilience in the minors.

Inexplicably, the Houston Astros, Cleveland Indians, Montreal Expos, Baltimore Orioles and Cincinnati Reds all passed on Jeter, whose fabulous senior season of baseball at Kalamazoo Central High School earned him accolades like top high school player in 1992 by the American Baseball Coaches Association.

Astros scout and Hall of Fame pitcher Hal Newhouser was so angry that the Astros didn't listen to his advice that he quit after they chose outfielder Phil Nevin instead. Cleveland passed because Jeter had suffered an ankle injury in his senior year and their scouts only saw limited at-bats. The Tribe tabbed University of North Carolina lefty Paul Shuey.

Focused on college pitchers, the Expos drafted Mississippi State's B.J. Wallace. The Orioles had Jeter as its highest-rated high schooler but selected Stanford's Jeffrey Hammonds.

It was between the Reds and the Yankees, and despite the advice of Gene Bennett, the scout who discovered Barry Larkin, Paul O'Neill and Eric Davis, the club chose University of Central Florida outfielder Chad Mottola.

The Reds' scouting director, Julian Mock, told *Newsday*'s Steven Marcus: "We had a Hall of Fame shortstop in the making [Larkin]. We needed a power outfielder and that's the reason we passed on [Jeter]."

The Yankees were overjoyed. "A cheer immediately went up in the Yankee Draft room in Tampa, one loud enough to echo across the Bronx," Ian O'Connor wrote in *The Captain: The Journey of Derek Jeter*. "Fists were pumped and backs were slapped. Somehow, some way, Derek Jeter had made it unscathed to the sixth pick."

A few weeks later, though overjoyed to be going to the team he had rooted for, Jeter—who had been described as "a young colt" by then-Montreal scout Dave Littlefield—struggled mightily. He didn't hit, was clumsy in the field and was homesick. But instead of sulking, he worked, and worked and worked. That's probably why he was promoted to Single-A Greensboro in 1993.

Offensively, he responded, hitting .295 with a .376 OBP. He wasn't hitting for power yet, but the hard work had paid off. In the field, however, he was still awful, making 56 errors.

Michael, who also made 56 errors in his year of minor-league ball, wasn't concerned. "When I saw him making all the errors, it really wasn't much of a concern with me," Michael told *Newsday*'s Barbara Barker. "I had watched him and he was really athletic and had really good hands. Sometimes he was erratic and he would hurry, but I wasn't worried."

Jeter once again showed the front office that he was committed to excellence. Right after the season, he went to the Instructional League and worked for six weeks with coach Brian Butterfield. "Butterfield changed the way Jeter threw (shortening his arm swing so that he didn't drop the ball below his waist) and the way he caught (showing him how to "take" the baseball rather than always catching it with "give")," wrote Tom Verducci for *Sports Illustrated*.

Jeter's 1994 began with Class A Tampa, then Double-A and, finally, Triple-A. His totals for the season were excellent, .344/.410/.463 with an OPS of .873. He would start the 1995 season in Triple-A and get a callup to the Yankees on May 29 to fill in for an injured Fernandez.

Jeter went 0-for-5 in his first game, but Yankee manager Buck Showalter told reporters after the game that he and the staff would take Jeter's stay one game at a time. "I don't want to get into what Derek has to do to stay up. We want him to relax and do what he's capable of doing. We hope Derek makes us a better club."

There are those who say Derek Jeter wasn't a good fielder. Then there those who saw him play every day and know better. *Photo by Bill Menzel.*

He didn't light the world on fire but had his share of nice flashes before he was demoted after thirteen games.

The next season would make Derek Jeter a household name. "We had a lot of guys who were valuable," said Torre of Jeter's 1996 season. "I don't think we had one guy, player-wise, who was more valuable than him."

I watched a lot of Yankee baseball in 1996, my first year of working in sports media. I figured that, as a Met fan, it would behoove me to cover the Yankees. I knew I could objectively cover the Mets, because I was harder on them than your average pom-pom waver. I just thought it made sense. No one knew me in the Bronx, and I would have a fresh start. I had been working as a producer on a radio station in Stamford, Connecticut (see chapter 1), and was given the chance to write and record a few sports stories.

Thanks to his slash line of .314/.370/.430 with an OPS of .800, including 10 homers, 78 RBIs and 104 runs scored in 157 games, Jeter was the unanimous choice for AL Rookie of the Year. He was such a refreshing change to how the Yankees usually operated: collecting big-name talent that didn't always pay off. He was only twenty-two but conducted himself like a professional well beyond his years.

"[Derek Jeter] wasn't the most talented player I ever covered, he wasn't the best interview, he wasn't the most charismatic. But no one came close to his ferocity, and I don't mean in just those big moments in October," wrote columnist Bob Klapisch. "Watch Jeter run out a ground ball on any night in midsummer, the ninth inning of a nothing game, and you understood what drove him."

I was so impressed with how Jeter responded to the pressure of his first postseason. He was the first Yankee first-round pick to play October baseball since Thurman Munson did in 1976. Jeter hit .361/.409/.449 and did so on the national stage. Jeter didn't do it on his own, but being a rookie, playing the game with toughness and smiling all through it, certainly made him stand out.

He had the tenacity of a Billy Martin, wrapped in the elegance of a Joe DiMaggio. That's how I would describe him.

He wouldn't be named the captain of the team until several years later, but his leadership was evident from the beginning. "Leadership is something that evolves; you don't walk into a clubhouse and say, 'Hey, I'm here, follow me'," Torre told YES Network's Lou DiPietro.

It doesn't happen right away, but Jeter was very unusual to be, at a young age, so responsible and comfortable in his own skin. The first playoff game we had against Texas, I think he made an error and we lost, and I was asked by the media if I felt I had to talk to him—being a rookie and all—and I said I'd figure it out. But on his way out of the clubhouse, he peeked into my office and said, "Mr. Torre, get your rest tonight, tomorrow's the most important game of your life," and I knew I didn't need to talk to him.

Jeter had his best season in 1999. Just twenty-five, he had a career-high 219 hits with 24 home runs and 102 RBI. He hit .349/.438/.552 with a .989 OPS during the regular season and a 1.001 in the postseason, helping the Yankees to a four-game sweep over the Braves.

He followed up that performance by slashing .339/.416/.481 with an .896 OPS in 2000 and then proceeded to slash .409/.480/.864 with a 1.344 OPS en route to winning the World Series MVP by beating the Mets in 2000.

On June 4, 2003, George Steinbrenner named Jeter the eleventh captain in team history, ironically making the announcement on the road in Cincinnati, the home of one of the teams that had passed on drafting Jeter back in 1996.

In one of his better missives, Big Stein channeled General Douglas MacArthur, "There is no substitute for victory....My gut tells me this would be a good time for Derek Jeter to assume leadership. He is a great leader by the way he performs and plays. I told him I want him to be the type of cavalry officer who can sit in the saddle. You can't be a leader unless you sit in the saddle. I think he can."

After the Yankees' shocking loss to the Florida Marlins in the 2003 World Series—in which Jeter slashed .346/.393/.462—Steinbrenner was livid. "Of course I was disappointed, but we will be meeting soon to make whatever changes are needed to bring back a stronger, better team for New York and our fans," Steinbrenner said in a statement after the Series. "You can count on it."

The 2003–4 offseason was a whirlwind for the Yankees. First, they let Andy Pettitte leave via free agency to sign with Houston; signed Gary Sheffield, Kenny Lofton and Tom "Flash" Gordon; and traded for Kevin Brown and Javier Vasquez.

But then they pulled the trigger on Alex Rodriguez. "George Steinbrenner is the center of evil in the universe," said Red Sox fan Ben Affleck, as his beloved team had a deal in place to get the All-Star shortstop before it was nixed by MLB.

The Yankees won the Al East again in 2004, but the Red Sox finally broke the Curse of the Bambino by storming back from a 3–0 deficit to win the pennant.

From 2005 to 2008, Jeter would slash .319/.390.449, win two Gold Gloves and three Silver Slugger Awards, but the Yankees could not replicate their previous success. Torre would get the blame after a 2007 ALDS ouster, and new skipper Joe Girardi would miss the postseason altogether in 2008.

Jeter had a remarkable 2009 regular season, slashing .334/.406/.465, and in the World Series he posted a .407/.429/.519 with three doubles to win his fifth and final world title.

It would be Jeter's last great season.

During Jeter's final playing days, some pundits and fans alike decided to spend the last few moments of the greatest shortstop in New York baseball history denigrating the once-dominant player, mocking his defense, which had deteriorated over the last years of his career.

After he decided to call it quits for the upcoming 2014 season, there were those who said that Jeter was not the great player that New York perceived him to be. For example, "If Jeter had played in Houston or Cincinnati, no one would know who he was."

Joe Morgan played in both Houston and Cincinnati. Ever heard of him?

"Derek Jeter is merely a very good player who benefited greatly from being drafted by the right team, at the right time, playing in the right city," wrote Tom Mechin for *Bleacher Report*. "Had he been drafted by any other team his legacy would be vastly different. For starters, he would not be as recognizable, nor as well-paid—both on and off the field—as he is. And he likely would not have spent the majority of his career surrounded and protected in a lineup filled with the game's best and highest paid players. Derek Jeter's greatness is more a matter of happenstance."

Happenstance? Jeter's career postseason batting line of .308/.374/.465 and an OPS of .838 isn't happenstance. Jeter ranks first in hits and plate appearances, games played, runs scored, total bases, singles and doubles, and he is tied for first in triples, third in home runs, fourth in RBIs, fifth in walks and sixth in stolen bases. Was he lucky to have had the ability to play for some great teams and be in a position to produce? Of course.

Here's the difference: He rose to the challenge.

ESPN's Keith Olbermann called Jeter overrated in 2014 and said he is not one of the top ten Yankees of all time, calling him "nowhere near an immortal."

Not one of the top ten Yankees of all time? He's number one in hits (3465), doubles (544), stolen bases (358) and games played (2,747), fourth in offensive WAR (96.3), fifth in position players WAR (72.4), eighth in batting average (.310) and I could go on and on.

Look. I've seen better defensive shortstops in my life—Ozzie Smith, Jeter's teammate Rodriguez and Omar Vizquel—but I don't remember Jeter ever costing his team the game in a big spot with an error. I know what the defensive metrics say (they say he was one of the worst defenders of his era), but most of Jeter's issues were due to his decreasing range over twenty years of playing the second-most-demanding position on the field next to catching.

Perhaps *Gotham Baseball* original John Sickels put it best. "As you also know, there's been a lot of controversy about Jeter's defense in recent years," Sickels wrote in 2013 for his *Minor League Blog*. "However, I find the whole topic of Jeter's glovework to be a tedious proxy for Yankee booster-ism and Yankee hatred....I'm just going to ignore it."

Over the years, I had several interactions with Jeter, always professional, at times aloof, but always consistent. I would have liked to have had at least one warm exchange with him before a game or made him laugh during a press conference, but it never happened.

That doesn't mean I don't miss him now that he's gone. Because I do. Didi Gregorious did a remarkable job taking over for Jeter at short for the Yanks, and he's a fun player to watch. But he's no Jeter, who finished just one vote shy of joining his teammate Rivera as the only unanimous inductees into Cooperstown.

Jeter didn't get to finish out his career as he began it, as a World Series champion, but his greatness shouldn't be measured by his last few years or his lack of a postseason curtain call or even how much money the Yankees sold his game-used socks for.

Greatness is measured by how he will be remembered, how even people who hate the Yankees will feel compelled to say how much they respected his career.

Me? I'll remember him for this quote, which sums up Jeter perfectly.

"The lights were always bright," Jeter wrote in his farewell to baseball on The Player's Tribune website. "The pace was always fast. The stakes were always high, and the expectations higher. And in those different memories—those moments that feel unique to New York—you always showed me a sign. Everybody comes to this city with dreams of being No. 1. You showed me that being No. 2 was more than enough."

15

DAVID WRIGHT

He had all the talent in the world, but what made David Wright special is that he never changed. He was always the same kid who wanted to learn and treated everyone—teammates, fans, security guards, clubbies, ticket takers—all the same. He's just a special person.
—Joe McEwing

The first time I heard the name David Wright, I was sitting in the outdoor press box at the Brooklyn Cyclones ballpark in Coney Island.

A few weeks earlier, on June 5, 2001, Wright had been selected by the Mets in the supplemental phase of the first round of the MLB Amateur Draft. At the time, I was doing a deep dive into the Met organization by covering the Cyclones' inaugural season. It gave me the unique opportunity to query the organizational folks who had been hanging around the team that summer.

"Great kid," said Gary LaRocque, who was then the Mets' director of scouting. "Mets fans are going to love him." That was the on-the-record portion of our conversation. Now that Wright is retired, I can add the off-the-record part.

"Are we going to see him here in Brooklyn?" I asked.

"Heck, no," he laughed.

When I asked him to explain, his response was unexpected. "I think being here would be a distraction for him, you guys [in the media] would be all over him, and we want him to concentrate on baseball. He's just eighteen," said LaRocque. "But we have really high hopes for him, he's special.

I took Gary at his word, and something told me to make it a point to track Wright's minor-league career moving forward.

Wright didn't have quite the high profile of Derek Jeter coming out of high school, but he did attract plenty of attention. Met scout (and former player) Randy Milligan was among several scouts who attended Wright's games in his senior year.

Milligan was very high on Wright and alerted former Met hitting coach Tom Robson, who at that time was a special assistant to then-GM Steve Phillips. "Robson kept telling us 'I love this kid from Virginia,'" Jim Duquette, a Met executive when the team drafted Wright, told me. "He said he liked him better than the other position players we were looking at."

Duquette said that Robson was insistent, even when he and the front-office staff pressed Robson about other players who were rated higher or more advanced college players. "We asked him, 'what about Khalil Green or Bobby Crosby?'" said Duquette. "But he just kept telling us, 'Nope, Wright's the guy.'"

When Wright joined the organization, it was clear he was there to do his job with enthusiasm. The scouts loved him, the coaches loved him and he had a solid debut season with the Kingsport Mets in the Rookie League, slashing .300/.391/.458 with an .850 OPS, 4 home runs and 17 RBIs in thirty-six games.

The following season, Wright was with the Low-A Capital City Bombers in the South Atlantic League, or the "Sally League," as it was called. Wright had some struggles in the more advanced league. He was just nineteen, and the big-league club was having a tough start to the season. GM Phillips was in the last year of his contract and was fighting for his job, and he actually offered Wright at that season's trade deadline in hopes of acquiring Blue Jay outfielder Jose Cruz Jr.

ESPN's Keith Law was working in the Toronto front office that year. "I was there when the call came in. It was the first time I'd heard of Wright, since I wasn't with Toronto in 2001 nor had I followed the draft when Wright was in it." wrote Law during a live chat. "[Blue Jays general manager] J.P [Ricciardi]'s reaction was, 'I'm not trading a major league player for some guy in the Sally League.' And that was pretty much that."

Crisis averted.

I've always made it a rule not to get too excited about a prospect until he hits Double-A. Most scouts agree that the jump from High-A ball to Double-A is the most difficult, but I have to admit, Wright's 2003 season with St. Lucie in the Florida State League (.270/.369/.459 with 15 home runs, 75 RBI, 19 stolen bases and an .828 OPS) got me excited. The FSL is a pitching-rich league; usually, hitters take a step back after the friendly confines of the Sally League.

As for the jump to Double-A, David answered that question pretty quickly, as he started the 2004 season with Double-A Binghamton, hitting .363 with 10 home runs and 40 RBIs in sixty games, which earned him a promotion to Triple-A Norfolk.

Duquette said there was a feeling among some of the other front-office staff that Wright could make the jump straight to the majors, while others thought giving Wright the chance to play in his hometown would be a nice way to progress.

Wright grew up a Met fan, attending games of their Triple-A farm team in Norfolk. He always wanted to play for them, even as a kid. In thirty-one games at Triple-A Norfolk, Wright hit .298 with 8 homers and 17 RBIs before he was called up. It was a risk to bring him up, Duquette told me, because the team had been struggling to get over .500 all season. "We were worried what the losing would do to him. Also, we had a different timetable for him, but he was such a special case, we said, 'Why not?'"

He struggled initially, hitting just .240 going into an August 5 game against the Brewers. But that day, he had a 6-RBI game that turned his season around. He would finish the season batting .293/.332/.525 with an .857 OPS, 14 homers and 40 RBIs in sixty-nine games.

For the next four seasons (2005–08), Wright was brilliant, hitting .311/.394/.534 with an OPS of .928. He averaged 158 games played, 29 home runs, 112 RBIs, 22 stolen bases, 42 doubles and 106 runs scored.

In 2006, he struggled in his first postseason, hitting just .160 against the Cardinals in the NLCS. But he would prove himself to be a clutch hitter while the rest of the team floundered during the consecutive choke jobs to blow a playoff spot in both 2007 and 2008. In 2007, Wright hit .352 with a 1.034 OPS in September; the following year, he hit .340 with a .993 OPS in the same scenario.

Hopes were high in 2009. The Mets' new ballpark, Citi Field, opened to rave reviews.

Ironically, while the exterior was built to look like Ebbets Field, the inside was anything but the hitter's paradise in Flatbush. The spacious outfield was highlighted by a 16-foot wall in left field, dubbed "The Great Wall of Flushing" by Mets broadcaster Howie Rose. The gap in right center, which at 371 feet had been a sweet spot for Wright at Shea Stadium, was 415 feet in the new ballpark.

If not for a few bad breaks, David Wright would have been a shoo-in for the Hall of Fame. *Photo by Bill Menzel.*

I toured the ballpark more than once while it was being constructed and asked several people if it had been tested to see how it would play. I wasn't smart enough to notice at the time how ridiculous the outfield dimensions were. (In 2011, the Mets admitted they had botched the construction of the ballpark and moved the fences in significantly. In 2015, they moved the right-center field wall in even more.)

Making matters even worse, Assistant GM Tony Bernazard, he of the career .262 batting average and .387 slugging percentage, implemented a new batting regimen for the Mets in 2009. Instead of building a park that would be neutral or even benefit their best player, the plan was now to hit to the opposite field. Everyone. On purpose.

Like a good soldier, Wright went along with this insanity. Manager Jerry Manuel and hitting coach Howard Johnson (who had been a dead pull hitter) were given the task of teaching the new technique.

Wright, who was just twenty-eight in 2010, had the worst season of his career to date: .254/.345/.427 with just 14 home runs and 61 RBIs. It would get worse. On August 15, San Francisco's Matt Cain hit Wright in the head, and while he did get back in September, the season would be a wash.

Overall, the Mets would lead the NL with a .270 batting average that year but slug just .394 and hit a pathetic 95 home runs, the fewest in the majors.

Wright bounced back in 2010 with 29 home runs, 103 RBIs and slashing .283/.354/.503 with an .856 OPS.

In April 2011, Wright was hurt trying to make a tag play at third. At first, it looked like a hamstring issue. However, Wright actually suffered a stress fracture in his lower back. He wouldn't get back until July and hit .272/.349/.440 with a .789 OPS for the rest of the season.

He was an All-Star again in 2012, and after the season, he signed an eight-year, $138 million deal that extended his contract. He was also named the fourth captain in team history.

That spring, he also became "Captain America," earning the deserving nickname after hitting .438 with a grand slam and 10 RBIs for Team USA in the World Baseball Classic. He ended the tourney early after a rib-cage injury but was upbeat with his new contract and new role.

"We think it's an honor few people get in the game, and certainly it's deserving," said manager Terry Collins. "He's not only the face of the organization, but I thought this past winter when he made the commitment, he wanted to be a New York Met forever, it was the right time."

Typical of Wright, he didn't wear a C on his jersey and told Collins and the organization that he didn't want the captaincy unless his teammates endorsed it.

He was enjoying what would be his last All-Star campaign in 2013 until a severe hamstring injury ended his season in August. A bad shoulder was the main reason for a terrible 2014 season, and after reinjuring his hamstring in 2015, he was diagnosed with lumbar spinal stenosis. He managed to get

Derek Jeter and David Wright, "Captain Clutch" and "Captain America," respectively. *Photo by Bill Menzel.*

back in time for the team's unlikely run to the 2015 NL pennant and the World Series and even hit a home run in Game 3 at Citi Field.

But his career was virtually over. He would get hurt again in 2016 and have season-ending surgery. He would try to get back for the 2017 season but was shut down in spring training. Finally, in 2018, he called it quits in an emotional farewell game on September 29. "We've had some pretty good times here and some rough years but you guys have always had my back and that means the world to me," he said in his postgame speech. "I wish I could thank everyone individually but all I can do is say thank you from the bottom of my heart.

"Thank you for letting me live out my dream here every single night."

I'm not crying, you're crying.

Wright deserved a better fate, to be sure. He was the total package, a five-tool guy with a personality, the face of the franchise.

"It was an honor to be a witness to the way he played the game," said former Met pitcher and current broadcaster Ron Darling. "He played hard whether it was on a winning team or losing team, he played the game the way it's supposed to be played. He's a pro's pro."

I've always admired Darling, because he's always been a gentleman. Be it for an interview for *Gotham Baseball* magazine when he was named to the SNY broadcast team or socially, Darling never gives anyone the high hat.

During our chat in the Mets' media dining room, I told Darling that he reminded me of Wright. When he looked at me quizzically, I added that they came from similar backgrounds and each had been brought up to respect people no matter their station in life. "Wow, I've never even thought about that, but wow, we do have a lot in common," nodded Darling. "My dad was in the Air Force and worked in a machine shop, his dad was a cop, so yes, blue-collar guys. He's the oldest of three of four brothers. I'm the oldest brother, so yes, we probably share more than we think."

I need to make something clear: I made the decision to select David Wright as the best third baseman ever to play in New York long before the interview I had with him in September 2018, right before he said goodbye to the Mets and his baseball career. I wasn't swayed by his tearful farewell or the flood of memories that came with it. Nor did the fact that I have covered his career since his minor-league days play a role. Make no mistake, he is the epitome of what I love in a ballplayer.

But another Yankee third baseman was also under consideration. Not who you think, though.

"I would love to get in [to the Hall of Fame], but I understand that I made my own bed," Alex Rodriguez said on ESPN's *First Take* in January 2019. "So if I don't make it to the Hall of Fame, I can live with that. I will be bummed, it would suck and I can't believe that I put myself in this situation. But if that happens, I have no one to blame but myself."

Couldn't have written it better myself, Alex.

No, the Yankee on the ballot was Graig Nettles, a brilliant fielder and home-run hitter, a gamer who played baseball the way it should be played.

More than a few folks tried to convince me that he was the better choice. "Defense wins championships," said my pal Geoff Buchan, a fantasy baseball analyst. "Watch Nettles in the '78 Series. Wright was a better hitter at his peak, but his glove was just average. Nettles was outstanding, perhaps the best defensive third baseman since Brooks Robinson. Nettles led the AL in home runs in 1976, a tougher era for hitters."

Ironically, Yankee fan Anthony Auspelmyer disagreed. "Both were the heartbeat of their team, but Wright gets the best of Nettles in most offensive categories including OPS+ (Wright's is 133, Nettles's is 114 as a

Yankee)," said Auspelmyer. "Both have two Gold Gloves, but Wright also has two Silver Sluggers (awarded annually to the best offensive player at each position). Nettles had an electric glove and the pedigree of a champ, but I have to go with Wright."

I asked WFAN's Howie Rose, a Met broadcaster since 1995, what he thought. "I want to be careful not to shortchange Nettles," Rose told me at Citi Field before a game in September 2018. "He was an incredibly good defensive third baseman. Just like Roger Maris, a uniform number [9] and a generation before, Nettles was the perfect Yankee Stadium hitter. Graig was a fabulous player, but he was never on a Hall of Fame track, where David Wright was."

Rose says that Wright gets the edge because of what Wright means to the Mets as their captain and as the face of the franchise. "He was asked to go so far above and beyond and being the conduit between the fans and the team. I would say that David transcended the game in terms of his impact on the franchise."

End of the day for me was that, while Nettles was the superior glove man, his slash line over eleven seasons (1,535 games) as a Yankee—.253/.329/.433 with an OPS of .762, 250 home runs and 834 RBIs—doesn't measure up to Wright's. David's fourteen-year Met career (1,585 games) resulted in a slash line of .296/.376/.491 with an .867 OPS with 242 homers and 970 RBIs.

As far as the balloting, Wright got 89.22 percent of the vote for third base, the highest vote total on the entire ballot. The other highest vote totals were Mariano Rivera (85.33 percent), Babe Ruth (84.94 percent) and Jackie Robinson (83.6 percent).

This certainly sums up the kind of guy David Wright is.

I called him a few days before his final game to interview him for this book. I knew he would be busy, and I also knew he'd be impossible to get one-on-one at Citi Field. "Hey, David, it's Mark Healey. I used to run *Gotham Baseball* magazine, thanks again for making some time for me today."

"Sure, I remember you, Mark," said Wright. "You guys put me on the cover of the magazine. I still have that in my office. I hope you'll send me a signed copy of the book when it's published."

Full disclosure, if I hadn't made up my mind many months before, *that* may have swayed me. But it didn't. That's just David being David—the best third baseman in New York baseball history.

16

MARIANO RIVERA

Mo has done things that nobody else in the history of the game has done. We wouldn't have the success we've had without him. Only a few teams in history have had the luxury of having someone they can count on every single day. He's been pretty much automatic.
—*Derek Jeter*

It's a beautiful spring day in the Bronx in 2006. Though hours before game time, there's a smattering of fans, young and old, gathered around the Yankee dugout. All are wearing some form of the classic interlocking "NY" logo; all are hoping to get an autograph, perhaps a wave or, at the very least, a smile from one of their pinstriped heroes.

The normally reserved players are in a relatively good mood. The Yankees had beat the Blue Jays in a solid 3–1 win the night before, and they oblige the fans by signing a few balls.

Then, he emerges.

He's only coming out of the dugout to take part in a photo shoot, but the small gathering is immediately silent and begins to clap that slow clap that one sees in sports movies. Though sometimes corny on celluloid, this entrance is as exciting to them as his trot from the bullpen in a tight ballgame. His simple action of walking out onto the sun-splashed Yankee Stadium grass is a theatrical event. His uniform gleams in the bright light, and its majesty is matched only by his easy smile as he stretches out his hand and asks me, "What do you need me to do?"

All these years later, I can remember every moment of that day. I had spent a few weeks trying to convince then-PR director of the Yankees, Rick Cerrone, to persuade Mariano Rivera to agree to pose for the front cover of *Gotham Baseball*.

Cerrone, who is now editor-in-chief at *Baseball Digest*, had been helpful when *Gotham Baseball* debuted the year before, but this was a huge favor. Players don't often consent to in-season photo shoots unless it's *Sports Illustrated*. But Rick said, "I'll ask."

A few days later, Rick said it was a go.

"What do you need me to do?" asked Rivera.

I told him to just pose in the "set" position. He obliged, albeit with a grin.

"No smiles," I jokingly scolded him.

"Okay," he answers. I could tell he complied reluctantly.

After a moment, he stopped grinning and finally stared that stare at the camera. The sudden change in his appearance was abrupt, and for a moment, both myself and the photographer shuddered—just a little.

We had just gotten a taste of what's it's like to be an opposing batter in the box against the "Hammer of God."

Thirty-one years earlier, a skinny little shortstop went to the pitcher's mound to help out his teammates. A major-league scout just happened to be at that game, and just $3,000 later, Mariano Rivera became a New York Yankee. It was an event that would later change the fortunes of a once-proud but languishing franchise. And, like the selection of Derek Jeter (who was passed over by five other teams), it might never have happened.

Born on November 29, 1969, in Panama City, Panama, Rivera wasn't even a pitcher when Yankee scout Herb Raybourn watched him stroll to the rubber from his position at shortstop. Raybourn, Panama's most famous baseball personality (at that time, anyway), was alone in his belief that the young son of a fisherman from La Chorrera had magic in his right arm.

The Yankees listened, and the scout who also discovered Ramiro Mendoza for New York had not only signed a Hall of Fame player but also the standard by which all closers are—and will be—judged.

It would take nearly six seasons for the young right-hander to make it to the major leagues, but as the big-league club slogged its way through the early '90s, the young Rivera was putting up superb minor-league stats, throwing just one pitch, a fastball that was topping out at around eighty-nine to ninety-one miles per hour.

Many things are remarkable about Rivera's early career, but consider this: Without a single effective breaking pitch or changeup, relying solely on command, he posted WHIP numbers of 0.46, 1.21 and 0.76 in 1990, 1991 and 1992, respectively.

That's just not fair.

As happens in every young pitcher's career, regardless of the numbers, someone comes along and says, "You need another pitch, son." Rivera agreed, as the young man was respectful of his elders and was eager to please. The result (and the culprit has never been identified) was that Rivera fiddled with his arm slots, which caused severe damage to his elbow.

However, as crazy luck would have it, the surgery came at the best time for the Yankees and Rivera. Because of the severity of the injury, he was left unprotected in the 1992 expansion draft, and neither the Florida Marlins nor the Colorado Rockies selected him.

After a successful rehab in 1993, Rivera—still with just one pitch—spent the next two seasons picking up where he had left off. He finished his minor-league career with the following stat line: 30-18, 2.34 ERA, 421 strikeouts and just 106 walks over 495⅔ innings. With one pitch. And it wasn't even *the* pitch. Not yet.

His fastball had matured, surely, and was now topping out at ninety-two miles per hour, but, except slipping in an occasional slider and "change-up," his main pitch was the high riser. In the spring of 1995, Rivera was nothing more than a solid twenty-five-year-old rotation prospect. Even with all of those dominant numbers, there were those in the Yankee hierarchy who were not very high on Rivera. In fact, some of them were urging Yankee GM Gene Michael to deal Rivera to the Detroit Tigers, who were dangling David Wells. But as Buster Olney wrote in June 2004 for *New York* magazine, Michael was not positive it was the right decision:

> On a June morning, Yankees general manager Gene Michael checked the reports from the minor-league games the night before and was stunned by what he saw: Pitching for Class AAA Columbus, Rivera was said to have thrown his fastball consistently at 95 mph, occasionally nicking 96. Michael didn't believe the readings and phoned the Columbus coaching staff to make sure their radar gun wasn't broken. No, they assured him, the radar gun was fine.
>
> Still skeptical, Michael phoned Jerry Walker, the Tigers scout who had been following Rivera—disguising the true purpose of his call by making small talk. By the way, Michael eventually asked Walker, how fast did you have Rivera throwing? Ninety-five miles per hour, consistently, Walker reported, touching 96. Michael cut off trade talks for Rivera. There must be something more in him, Michael thought, that we are just starting to see.

One pitch, discovered by chance, made Mariano Rivera the best closer in history. *Photo by Bill Menzel.*

Later that year—on July 4, to be exact—Rivera made his most impressive start of the season. It came against Chicago, when he struck out eleven in a two-hit shutout at Comiskey Park.

As the season went along, Showalter saw enough of Rivera's velocity and command to include him on the postseason roster, and though he was far from the dominator he would become, he gave a brief flash of what was to be.

In nine relief outings that season, most of them down the stretch, he went 2-0 with a 4.24 ERA, allowing just 8 hits over 17 innings. Yet Showalter didn't trust him quite enough, and as *New York Post* columnist Joel Sherman recounts in his excellent *Birth of a Dynasty*:

> *Consider: In spring training 1996, incumbent shortstop Tony Fernandez suffered a serious injury. Chief scout Clyde King insisted an erratic*

21-year-old prospect named Derek Jeter was not ready for the major leagues. Yankees officials mulled a Seattle offer of [journeyman shortstop Felix] Fermin for either Bob Wickman or the pitcher that had so impressed the Mariners in the Division Series the previous October: Mariano Rivera. On March 26, 1996, this possibility existed: Rivera would be traded to Seattle and Jeter demoted to Columbus. A dynasty was teetering, and no one knew it.

Even as late as early 1996, new Yankee manager Joe Torre wasn't sure what role Rivera would fill going into the season, telling the *New York Daily News* that Rivera "needed a change-up."

"To be a starter, he has to have a change," said Torre, who believed that Rivera would spend the 1996 season as a swingman, not as a setup man or a starter. To their credit, Torre and his coaches realized quickly that Rivera's arm was a weapon of mass destruction, and he complied, striking out 130 batters over 107.7 innings and allowing just 1 home run.

While he was impressive enough, it's still mind-boggling to think that the Yankees—yes, the New York Yankees—went into the 1997 season with a relatively unproven pitcher as their closer, letting World Series MVP John Wetteland leave in the process.

No one, not even Rivera, seemed worried about the upcoming season. "I was happy with what I was doing, so I went back to Panama after the World Series and assumed I would be the setup man again, which I was excited about," Rivera told mlb.com. "Then I got a call from the team, telling me that Wetteland wasn't coming back and that they were going to make me the closer. I told them I'd be there."

It didn't start out smoothly, as Rivera's first month as a closer started to look like his last, blowing four saves alone in April. "I was young and had never done it before," Rivera said. "I asked a lot of myself and beat myself up a lot when I didn't do my job."

It was around this time that he discovered the cutter. Now, depending on who you believe, either Yankee pitching coach Mel Stottlemyre, on orders from Torre, went out of his way to teach Rivera cutters or did so by accident while playing catch with Mendoza.

Rivera, who was very close with his countryman, was trying to throw the ball straight, but the ball kept sliding to Mendoza's right. "Mendoza got upset with me, but the ball just moved," Rivera says. "A few days later in Detroit, we tried it off the mound, and we couldn't straighten out the pitch. So, we said, 'Let's see what happens when we throw it in a game.'"

The heavy cutter transformed a hard-throwing setup man to the most dominant closer the game has ever known.

Even his failure in that year's ALDS against Cleveland—Sandy Alomar Jr. hit a game-tying home run off him in Game 4, and the Indians later won the game and the series in five games—couldn't overshadow his immense talent.

The next season, arguably one of the best in Yankee history, was Rivera's real coming-out party.

In 1998, Rivera would become the most dominant closer in the game, saving 36 games in 41 opportunities, allowing only 48 hits in 61⅓ innings pitched. In the World Series, he was brilliant against the San Diego Padres, posting three saves and a 0.00 ERA.

He saved 45 of 49 games during the regular season in 1999, threw 12 scoreless innings in the playoffs and earned his first World Series MVP against the Braves. "It's hard enough to hit a guy throwing ninety-five miles per hour. But to hit a guy throwing 95 miles per hour with eight inches of cut? That's why it's an eight-inning game for them," Braves third baseman Chipper Jones said of Rivera.

His MVP trophy was evidence of how much Rivera meant to the Bombers, who lacked a 20-game winner or a 30-homer hitter.

In 2000, Mariano made appearances in all four World Series wins for the Yankees against the crosstown Mets, earning saves in Games 4 and 5.

Then came the 2001 World Series, which showed that, while Rivera was still the best closer in baseball, he was human. Not that he pitched badly, mind you, but it looked like even the Hammer of God was subject to a little Murphy's Law once in a while.

Misplays behind him and a bloop hit beat him in Game 7 of that World Series, and in the ALDS loss of 2002 and the World Series defeat of 2003, Rivera played little role at all.

Then came 2004 and the "Reverse of the Curse."

It was unthinkable. The Yankees held a 3–0 series lead and asked Mariano to come into the eighth inning in Game 4 with the Yankees leading, 4–3. He got out of the eighth and needed just three outs to send the Yankees right back to the World Series.

Rivera walked Kevin Millar to begin the ninth, and Dave Roberts pinch-ran for Millar. Roberts stole second, and Bill Mueller's single scored Roberts. Boston would later win it in the twelfth inning and would win the next three games to post the first comeback from a 3–0 deficit, making Yankee fans questioning everything that offseason.

The hangover was still hurting the next April, because a rough start to the season and another blown save to the Red Sox brought boos from the Yankee Stadium crowd.

It also drew this column by MSNBC.com's Mike Celizic:

> *Something is wrong with Mariano Rivera. Not something little, but something big, something that could spell the end of his long reign as the best big-game closer in the game.*
>
> *What's more, the Yankees know that Rivera is no longer what he was; that he hasn't been that unhittable freak, the Sandman, for quite some time.*

Well, so much for that theory there, Mike. But thanks for playing.

He wasn't alone, as athomeplate.com blogger Daniel Paulling wrote the following at the start of the 2005 season:

> *Ralph Branca, 1951. Donnie Moore, 1986. Mitch Williams, 1992. Billy Koch, 2002. All four of these pitchers served up homers and lost big games. Branca gave up the "Shot heard 'round the world." Donnie Moore killed himself three years later. Mitch Williams pitched 37 more innings the rest of his life. Billy Koch is out of baseball. Mariano Rivera, 2004? Perhaps.*

Um, actually, no. Perhaps not.

Despite the catcalls and the doomsayers, Rivera posted another brilliant 1.38 ERA, saved 43 games and went 7-4 on the season. He allowed just 1 hit and 1 run over three innings of the 2005 ALDS defeat to the Angels and tossed one scoreless inning of the first-round debacle against the Tigers in 2006.

After the 2007 season, I wrote: "Rivera has been dominant for so long, it's hard to imagine that his tenure with the Yankees will end someday, but end it will. If this past year is Rivera's last really good year, you still owe it to yourself to watch him pitch as much as you can this in 2008. You'll never see anyone else as good ever again."

Little did I know that Rivera had many more pitches left in his right arm.

From 2008 to 2011, Rivera averaged 40 saves and 64 strikeouts in 65 innings, a 1.71 ERA, a 2.47 FIP and a WHIP of 0.821. It was ridiculous watching him pitch.

After the World Series in 2009, which I covered for *Baseball Digest*, it was hard to comprehend, but the man I watched get the final five outs against the Philadelphia Phillies to win the title was every bit the pitcher at thirty-nine that he had been at twenty-nine, and in some cases even better.

"All of them are great, but this one is special," Rivera said after the game. "It was a drought for nine years and we finally got one."

It would be the last World Series appearance for Mariano, but there would be stories left to tell.

The next two seasons were Rivera-esque, and he wouldn't allow an earned run in the 2010 and 2011 postseasons. It looked like Mariano was invincible.

Then, this happened:

> *But that legendary calm was shattered Thursday afternoon as Rivera lay on the warning track at Kauffman Stadium after sustaining a devastating knee injury that could signal the end of his remarkable career.*
>
> *Rivera, 42, tore the anterior cruciate ligament in his right knee while chasing a fly ball during batting practice before the Yankees' game against the Royals. As he ran toward the center-field wall, his knee buckled and he crashed into the wall, then fell to the warning track dirt, clutching his right knee as he grimaced in pain.*
>
> *During the game Rivera was taken to Kansas University MedWest hospital for a magnetic resonance imaging test and Royals team physician, Dr. Vincent Key, provided a diagnosis of the torn A.C.L., which almost certainly means Rivera has thrown his last pitch of the season, if not his career.*

The dramatic story was written by the *New York Times*' David Waldstien, and the headline "Rivera Hurts Knee; Career May Be Over" had so many people believing that Rivera's career was over and some even started talking about Rivera in the past tense.

I don't know why, but I knew in my heart that Rivera was not going to allow that to be his last moments in a Yankee uniform. Perhaps it was because I remembered what my good friend Gary Armida had written about Rivera for *Gotham Baseball*:

> *He isn't brash like Muhammad Ali, shouting that he's the greatest. He doesn't have the marketing campaign like Michael Jordan once had with Nike and Gatorade. He doesn't have people singing to be like Mo. He doesn't even have the marketing appeal of his teammate, Derek Jeter. When people rank the best players in baseball, his name is rarely mentioned as most gravitate towards the hitter. But, that feeling when he is on the mound is every bit as powerful as Ali in the ring hanging on the ropes right before he knocks out George Foreman. It is every bit as*

powerful as Michael Jordan taking a jump shot as the clock counts down to zero and his team down by one. It is the feeling of inevitability.

Inevitability is what separates the good from legend. It was inevitable that Ali would win. Michael Jordan was going to make the shot. We knew that going into the event. We watched anyway, getting a glimpse at a rare athlete in his prime able to control his opponents, himself, and the sport. That is Mariano Rivera, even at age 41. It is inevitable that Rivera will finish the game with the same pitch he has been throwing for nearly two decades. For a while, everyone was waiting for him to fail, to fall off that perch, and to become human. It happened to Ali. Even Michael Jordan looked human in Washington. Rivera is different. He isn't slowing down; he doesn't have any signs of being a mortal reliever. The only concessions to age have been a slower start in the Spring and less multi-inning appearances. Other than those, Rivera is still the standard.

The last man to wear number 42 was Mariano Rivera. *Photo by Bill Menzel.*

In 2014, his last season, at age forty-three, Rivera pitched 64 innings, walked just 9, struck out 54, had an ERA of 2.11, a FIP of 3.05 and a WHIP of 1.05. Inevitable? More like unanimous. As in January 2019, when Mariano Rivera became the first player elected unanimously to the Baseball Hall of Fame. Not Babe Ruth, not Willie Mays, but Mariano. Ken Griffey Jr. nearly missed that distinction in 2016 (99.3 percent), and in 1992, Tom Seaver was on 98.8 percent of ballots.

"After my career, I was thinking that I had a shot to be a Hall of Famer," Rivera said on a conference call with reporters after learning the news. "But this was just beyond my imagination. I was amazed the way all this has been, through my whole career—and this being the pinnacle of every player that plays the game of baseball, to be unanimous."

After closing out so many games for manager Joe Girardi, the usually stoic skipper tearfully closed out Mariano's last game with this emotional farewell: "He made my job fun. He made my job easy. And he made all of our lives better."

17

JOE TORRE

The game belongs to the players. I'm one of those managers that likes to stay out of the way and let the players play. I think it certainly gives the fans a better show, and it gives them a lot more freedom.
—*Joe Torre*

After a devastating loss to the Seattle Mariners in the 1995 American League Divisional Series, Yankees manager Buck Showalter and GM Gene Michael were out of a job.

Despite the two men's efforts in building and developing an overachieving team that had earned MLB's first-ever AL wildcard berth, principal owner George Steinbrenner couldn't get past the fact that his team had lost to the Mariners.

Despite a heroic last gasp of excellence by Don Mattingly (who hit .417, including his only postseason home run), the Yankees had blown a 2–0 series lead, squandered a 5–0 lead in Game 4 and lost the series at the dreadful Kingdome despite leads of 4–2 and 5–4, eventually losing in the eleventh inning.

At this point, even though Mariano Rivera had closed out Game 2 with three and one-third strong innings to earn the win (his first postseason victory ever), he was still a rookie who had sported a 5.50 ERA during the 1995 regular season. Instead, it was "Black Jack" McDowell on the bump when Edgar Martinez drove home the winning run.

Sportswriter Jack Curry, who chronicled the series for the *New York Times*, wrote this little tidbit at the end of his column:

> *Steinbrenner paraded around the clubhouse after the game and shook hands with players. Surprisingly calm, Steinbrenner said he was "proud" of the Yankees and that "the frustration will set in later." He declined to discuss the futures of Manager Buck Showalter or General Manager Gene Michael, whose contracts are up at the end of the month. "Let's not start any of that," said Steinbrenner. "Let's stay where we are here and now."*

In his excellent book *Birth of a Dynasty*, about the 1996 Yankees, Joel Sherman wrote: "Michael and Showalter…were in Steinbrenner crosshairs throughout 1995. They had committed a Yankees sin in the age of Steinbrenner, they were getting far too much credit. 'If we had just won against the Mariners we all would have been fine,' Michael said."

But they didn't win, and on October 23, Bob Watson was the new GM. On November 2, Torre was introduced as the new manager of the Yankees.

In his masterwork *Pinstripe Empire*, Marty Appel says that Michael was the first to suggest that Torre would be a good fit with the Yankees. The idea was seconded by Yankee advisor Arthur Richman, who at one time had been the traveling secretary when Torre was with the Mets. "He was my choice and he was Watson's choice," said Michael to Murray Chass of the *New York Times* after the press conference at Yankee Stadium. "He's good with the players; he's open and honest with them. He's handled this market before. I think he can continue to do that."

Very much like when no one was paying much attention when Michael remade the Yankees with many of the metrics Oakland's Billy Beane "invented" a decade later, most of the reaction to the Torre hiring appeared to ignore what would be prophetic commentary by Michael. In fact, the blowback to the decision was so negative, Steinbrenner tried to get Showalter back, meeting with Buck a week after the Torre press conference.

Torre handled that awkward period as deftly as he would handle the next twelve years. "It was good for my ego to be named the Yankee manager." Torre told Sherman in *Birth of a Dynasty*. "I tried not to think about [how Steinbrenner went after Buck afterward]. I knew the [Buck] had won for him."

I had a different feeling than most when Torre was hired by the Yankees, because I had a little perspective. Rocco Torre, Joe's oldest brother, lived in my neighborhood, I worked at the local video store, and Rocco would come in two or three times a week to rent movies, and we'd talk baseball.

Rocco, who spent more than thirty years as a New York police officer and an agent of the Drug Enforcement Administration (DEA), would call me "Markle," and he'd yell it when he walked in the door. One time, he came in with a box that contained these beautiful, brand-new sneakers, and he said, "Markle, my brother gave these to me. I'll never wear them. They're yours."

Sometimes, he'd come in with his wife, Rose, a very nice lady, and ask me to recommend movies for them to watch.

He would often ask me what I thought of his brother, and I told him the truth as I saw it as a fan.

I had mixed feelings about Torre when he was the Mets' manager from 1977 to 1981. I loved that he was a Brooklyn guy, loved that he was Italian and especially liked how articulate he was.

On June 1, 1977, Torre—who as a player had been traded to the Mets in 1975—replaced Joe "Cobra" Frazier as manager of the Mets after the team had started the season 15-30. Technically, he was a "player-manager," but he'd been a shell of the borderline Hall of Fame hitter he'd once been.

The club he took over was embroiled in turmoil. The long-standing feud between team chairman M. Donald Grant and star pitcher Tom Seaver had been simmering all spring, and the team's best power hitter, Dave Kingman, wanted a new deal.

In his first press conference after getting hired, Torre told the *Daily News'* Red Foley: "[I hope] Tom Seaver and Dave Kingman change their minds about wanting to leave the club. My office is open to them."

Open or not, both would be gone just two weeks later.

Ultimately, what I didn't like about Torre was how he could be so calm with a team that lost ninety-six (1978), ninety-nine (1979) and ninety-five (1980) games in each of his first three full seasons.

We talked about this, and Rocco explained—very patiently—exactly the hand his brother had been dealt. "They never gave him any players," he said.

The Mets had the lowest payroll in the NL East during Torre's tenure and were consistently in the bottom third of payroll in both leagues.

Then there were the drugs. According to Rocco, who was retired NYPD and had worked with the DEA, several players on those teams had severe drug problems. "Don't be too hard on my brother," Rocco would laugh. "That was the worst job."

I had lost touch with Rocco after I stopped working at the video store in 1991 and moved to California (see chapter 1), but those days spent with Rocco had really changed my perspective. So, I was a voice of reason to the Yankee fans among my family and friends in 1996.

The year I spent in Hollywood had also made me hungry for all things New York. My future wife and my mom had been sending me the newspapers from New York whenever they could (this was before the Internet), and when I came back, I paid nearly as much attention to the Yankees as I did the Mets. This would serve me well in the coming year, as the 1996 season was my first as a media professional.

While being more receptive to the idea of Joe Torre managing the Yankees, I still felt that Michael and Showalter seemed to have things well in hand. So, while I truly did not understand the move to hire Torre, I didn't share the "Clueless Joe" sentiment that most had about his ability or background. I felt knew better, I guess.

First off, I'm always amazed at how little has been written about Torre's tenure with the Mets, so I decided to take a closer look for this book. The Mets were already horrible to start 1977, so the fact that the shell-shocked team stumbled its way to a ninety-eight-loss season after the Seaver trade really couldn't be blamed on Torre.

Neither could 1978. The team went 10-15 in spring training, and despite a roster with little depth and even less talent than the year before, Torre was optimistic. "It was a very good spring," he told reporters. "What did we accomplish? I'll let you know in July."

After a 3-0 start, the team was 33-46 by July 1 and finished dead last.

In 1979, the year the Mets lost 99 games—its worst season since losing 101 games in 1967—the team lost 35 games by a single run, the worst in baseball. They also won just 28 games at Shea Stadium, the worst home-field performance in MLB that season. Only 788,905 fans showed up to watch that debacle of a year, the worst full-season attendance record in franchise history.

So it was Torre just being at the wrong place at the wrong time; it was the dark days of Met history. M. Donald Grant had been exiled in 1978, but the damage had been done.

The hope for Torre came when Nelson Doubleday came to town, ponied up $21.1 million and hired Frank Cashen. The 1980 Mets wouldn't win many games, either. Cashen didn't spend any of his new bosses' cash right away. And it showed. "I said before the [1980] season started that we'd have trouble scoring runs," Torre told *Sports Illustrated*'s Steve Wulf in the June 2, 1980 issue. "I'm sorry I was right."

That was also the season when the Mets managed just 61 home runs as a team, worst in MLB and the subject of a *Daily News* "Mets vs. Maris" item that ran daily.

Despite the terrible offense, players like Mookie Wilson, Wally Backman, Hubie Brooks and Neil Allen all got a chance to play. I remember how much I liked all of them, and I felt like 1981 could be special.

It almost was. After a midseason strike that would allow for two division winners at the end of the season, the Mets made a nice run toward the second-half NL East title with a 24-28 record. Maybe this Torre guy isn't so bad, I thought to myself.

Cashen fired him and his entire coaching staff at the end of the year, anyway. "It hurts your pride, Mike, if you have any pride, it hurts," Torre told *Eyewitness News* sportscaster Mike Barry. "You failed to do a job, which is what [I] was told, but you have to pick yourself back up, and that's what it amounts to. I felt it coming…when you take this job, it's going to happen eventually.…I'm just sorry because it looks like this team has a chance to win and I'm not going to be a part of it."

Torre was asked if he would manage again. "Yes, I plan to keep doing it until I get it right."

Torre would have his first brush with a megalomaniacal owner the very next season, as media mogul Ted Turner hired Torre to manage the Atlanta Braves. In the book *Joe Torre's Ground Rules for Winners*, he writes that Turner was far more intrusive than George Steinbrenner. "He was more of a problem than Steinbrenner has ever been."

During his three-year stint in Atlanta, Torre led the team to one divisional championship and a pair of second-place finishes, but Turner fired him after the 1984 season. Torre went into broadcasting, manning the booth for five seasons with the California Angels.

Torre did a fine job in St. Louis, notching winning records in his first three seasons, but he never reached the playoffs and had gotten off to a 20-27 start in 1995. New general manager Walt Jocketty was criticized by *St. Louis Post-Dispatch* columnist Bernie Miklasz, who said the Cardinals "dumped a classy guy, Torre, to feed the wolfpack.…All I see is a cheap PR move. All I see is a twitch reflex from a panic attack."

In retrospect, Torre was at the right place at the right time when Big Stein came calling. For most of his baseball life, Torre had been on the outside looking in.

Now he was with the Yankees.

Like one of his predecessors, Casey Stengel, Torre came to the Yankees with the reputation of being a less than effective manager. However, like the Ol' Perfesser, Torre became a master of his craft in the Bronx and will eventually joined Stengel in Cooperstown.

The only people who were clueless were Joe Torre's critics. *Photo by Bill Menzel.*

There are other similarities with Stengel. Each was a very good ballplayer in his day, though Torre was the far more powerful statistically. Each proved to be more than adept at dealing with the media. And each discovered that a strong bench would prove as valuable as the star players that littered their respective rosters.

Like Stengel, Torre's hiring was ridiculed by the cynical New York media. In 1949, they viewed Stengel as a jovial clown who they liked but didn't believe was an improvement over the popular Bucky Harris. In 1996, "Clueless Joe" was the media mantra.

In both cases, the press was quite wrong. Casey presided over seven World Series titles, ten AL pennants and only one season (1949; 79-74) in which the club failed to win at least ninety games. Most, including this reporter, believes Stengel's record will never be matched, as the now-illegal reserve clause and the lack of free agency allowed tightwad GM George Weiss to hold sway over his talented roster.

Torre, even with the biggest budget in baseball, managed the Yankees to a twelve-year span of superb baseball, better than any other franchise during that period. Contrary to popular belief, Torre not only knew what he was getting into but, perhaps more than any other Yankee manager who preceded him, was also more than prepared for the eccentricities that his new job would present him with.

The cockiness of the Reggie years were gone, the drama—at least inside the clubhouse—replaced by a steely professionalism. However, the retirement of Don Mattingly, the banishment of Mike Stanley (ironically, for Joe Girardi) and the sudden replacement of both Michael and Showalter created a very unpopular sentiment with the media and, by extension, the fanbase.

Despite those daunting odds, Torre was able to turn things around very quickly. An early-season slump for free agent first baseman Tino Martinez was compounded by the fact he was replacing Mattingly, who had retired after the 1995 season. Hearing cries of "Donnie Baseball" every time he came to bat during an April slump, Martinez had a harsh welcome to the Bronx.

Yet the calmness of Torre prevailed over any other emotion in the clubhouse. In another room, perhaps defensiveness or even anger at one's predicament would have boiled over. But not in Torre's clubhouse. Martinez got out of his slump and would finish the season with 117 RBIs.

The pitchers weren't immune either, as staff ace David Cone went down in May with an aneurysm in his right arm. Former Met Dwight Gooden threw a no-hitter against heavy-hitting Seattle about a week later.

On June 22, Torre learned that Rocco had died of a heart attack in between games of a doubleheader in Cleveland. It was hard not to root for Joe to do well with the Yankees after that. It was an emotional rollercoaster that would have weakened the resolve of any man, but Torre never let it affect his public demeanor.

Not only would Torre's thirty-five years of waiting for a World Series be over, but it also would come after beating the Braves, the team that signed him, traded him and then fired him.

The following year would prove to be far more difficult in terms of ultimate success, and the Yankees would win ninety-seven games, finish in second place in the AL East but fall short in the first round to the Cleveland Indians. Though it would mark the fourth time in twelve years that a Torre juggernaut was knocked off in the first round, it also set the stage for the greatest year of the Torre era.

The 1998 Yankees spent 135 days in first place and won their division by twenty-two games, and their skipper was named Manager of the Year.

"When I took this job a couple of years ago, it was questioned how could you work for George Steinbrenner," said Torre said in the celebratory press conference following the four-game sweep of the Padres in the 1998 Series. "But when you've been with different organizations that are only allowed to get so good, you appreciate the opportunity George gives you....George is going to find a way to fix it if it's broke."

The next season would prove as emotional—and, ultimately, as successful—as 1996, if not more so. The club learned in spring training that Torre was stricken with prostate cancer and, just a few days later, got the news that Joe DiMaggio had passed away. Though they would sweep another World Series, this time against the Braves, it would be a year of loss, as Scott Brosius, Luis Sojo and Paul O'Neill all lost their fathers.

It was an emotionally charged victory, but it wouldn't come close to the 2000 season, which would be the joyous calm before the storm.

Torre, to his credit, never billed it as such, but the win over the Mets in the 2000 World Series was the sweetest yet. Villainized all season by the tabloid media after Roger Clemens had beaned Mike Piazza in the second game of a day-night doubleheader, the Yankees geared up one last time to finish off Bobby Valentine's team.

I was not rooting for Torre that season, and that was easily the worst I've ever felt as a Mets fan.

It would also be the last World Series title for Torre and the Yankees during his tenure.

Torre and the Yankees returned to the World Series in 2001, helping heal the city after the September 11 terrorist attacks. But the team lost the Series to Arizona in seven games.

Over the next three years, the Yankees would set a club record by notching one-hundred-plus wins three seasons in a row, but each campaign would prove more disappointing than the next, culminating in the Yankees blowing a 3-0 lead in the ALCS to the Boston Red Sox.

The Red Sox? Yep. They didn't just reverse the Curse of the Bambino, they, as so eloquently put by Boston pitcher Pedro Martinez, drilled them "in the ass."

Not many managers would have been able to respond to that kind of collapse, especially when one's employer is Steinbrenner. But not even a cuddly Boss would have been as understanding as the years ensued. In 2005, the Angels knocked out the Yankees in five games. In 2006, the Yankees lost to the Tigers in four. And in 2007, the Indians won it in four as well.

Almost forgotten in the aftermath of the latest first-round debacle was the managing job that Torre did in 2007, which was perhaps his best ever. Facing a fourteen-and-a-half-game deficit in June, the Yankees not only made it all the way back to win the AL Wild Card spot, but they also made the Red Sox sweat the AL East lead until the last week of the season.

Still, the loss to the Tribe was too much for ownership to take. Torre quickly turned down the one-year offer that the team created for him to return, and within days, he joined the Los Angeles Dodgers.

So why is Torre the Gotham Legends manager?

This quote comes from William Tasker at the website Start Spreading the News: "Joe Torre was our calm in the storm. When all things Yankees flew around like fruit in a blender without the cover, he was unflappable. He was the rock with the press. He did not take any guff from George Steinbrenner. There was hardly ever a ruffle in his posture. I once made the joke that Joe Torre was the Ronald Reagan of managers. He made it look so easy that he could not have been that great."

Given how the front offices of baseball are now run, we may never see a manager like this again. That's a damn shame.

18

ED BARROW

Under Ed Barrow, one of the most complex and infinitely the most efficient baseball business firm ever operated was a one-man organization. Its central office was under Ed's hat.
—*Red Smith*

In an age when MLB's general managers have become the real power brokers for their respective clubs, the man who was considered baseball's first modern GM is still my pick for the best of all time: Edward Grant Barrow.

Barrow was a successful businessman and a minor-league manager who discovered Hall of Fame shortstop Honus Wagner, served as president of the International League and, in his first year of managing the Boston Red Sox, figured out that his star left-handed pitcher would be a better value to the team as a slugger.

Until Barrow came on board, Babe Ruth's hitting was relegated to the days he pitched. Ever a prima donna, he would complain during his first season that playing in the outfield was "boring," but Barrow stood up to his young star. Ruth would play a career-high ninety-five games in 1918, hit an MLB-best 11 of the Red Sox's 15 home runs that season and "only" pitch 166 innings—with a career-best 1.075 WHIP.

"Jidge," as he was called in Beantown, would also win two World Series games, helping Boston win its last championship until the 2004 team broke the Curse of the Bambino.

Ed Barrow, general manager. *Illustration by John Pennisi.*

Winning the Series was a great accomplishment, but because of America's entry into World War I, the profits that Red Sox owner Harry Frazee thought he was going to make never materialized. Ruth was his most valuable commodity, especially after he hit 29 home runs in 1919 and became baseball's biggest star.

Barrow was adamantly against the Sox moving Ruth to the Yankees following Boston's 66-71 season in 1919, and the Boston media—which has since whined and opined for decades about how stupid and gullible Frazee was—actually applauded the move in some circles.

When the Yankee owners then asked for Barrow to join their club as a front-office man the following season, Frazee happily complied. Which move was worse?

In Dan Levitt's excellent *Ed Barrow: The Bulldog Who Built the Yankees' First Dynasty*, he writes that "the Ruth purchase placed America's best baseball player and biggest sports celebrity in its largest city. The Barrow acquisition a year later ensured that the short-term boost from Ruth would be solidified and prolonged into one of the great sports dynasties of the 20th century."

At that time, most of the clubs in baseball kept their business and baseball separate, and the Yankees were no different. Bringing in Ruth cost the Yankee owners Jacob Ruppert and Tillinghast L'Hommedieu Huston a lot of money; $100,000 just to get him, and another $20,000 just to pay him for the 1920 season.

The two owners were constantly at odds, mostly over manager Miller Huggins, whom Ruppert had hired in 1918 without Huston's consent. The diminutive Huggins—who had been recommended by American League president Ban Johnson—had taken over a team that had finished in sixth place (71-82, 28.5 GB) in 1917. The team didn't have a winning year in 1918 (60-63 in a war-shortened season) but improved.

In 1919, things got even better, as the Yankees finished in third place (80-59, 7.5 GB). But Huston had little respect for Huggins and spent much of his remaining years as co-owner trying to undermine him at every step.

It was Huggins who suggested getting Ruth when the price tag seemed too high. So, when the Babe exploded for 54 home runs in 1920, helping the Yankees win ninety-five games, you'd think that Huggins would have gotten a reprieve. But the team finished in third place again, and the press was very critical, prompting Huston to try to force a change.

The pressure was so great that Huggins wrote a letter of resignation to Ruppert, who declined to accept it. Instead, Ruppert and Huston decided it was time to change the dynamic.

The Yankees' business manager, Harry Sparrow, had died in May 1920, making the two owners more involved in the day-to-day operations of the team, which neither wished to be. Once again, the pair looked to Boston and their friend Frazee and inquired about the availability of Barrow.

Though he had run a whole league and several businesses and was a manager, Barrow had never quite been given the reins before. Now, in addition to trying to get the Yankees to the next level, Barrow had more than one job. As business manager, he would have to run the day-to-day operations of the team, including Yankee Stadium. He had to mediate between the two owners and protect Huggins, making sure his only job was focusing on the club. "You are the manager, you will not be second-guessed by me," Barrow told Huggins. "Your job is to win, mine is to get you the players you need to win. I'll take responsibility for every deal I make."

Barrow's first target was his old club. He knew Frazee was desperate for cash and knew he wouldn't have to part with any real talent, so he was able to pick the Red Sox clean for the next half decade. His first few deals—adding Waite Hoyt, Herb Pennock, shortstop Everett Scott and third baseman Joe Dugan—were one-sided deals that made the Yankees back-to-back pennant winners in 1921 and 1922.

When the Yankees won their first World Series championship in 1923, half of their starting nine and five of their six best pitchers were ex-Boston players.

The true genius of Barrow was the ability to recognize the best way to acquire talent. Trading with the Red Sox was a limited exercise, so he convinced ownership that more full-time scouts were needed to maximize the team's investments in players.

So Barrow created the best scouting department in all of baseball, starting with one of his Boston coaches, Paul Krichell. Krichell's first signing? A strapping young first baseman from Columbia University named Lou Gehrig. After Krichell came Bill Essick and Joe Devine, who worked the West Coast and came up with a kid named Joe DiMaggio playing in San Francisco.

As Marty Appel wrote for *Yankees Magazine*:

> *You might think that only a fool would pass on Joe, who had had a 61-*
> *game hitting streak in 1933, but a knee injury the following year made*
> *every other club shy away from him. Only Essick and Devine said "sign*
> *him!" You don't need to be reminded how that one turned out. And with*
> *that signing, the reputations of Essick and Devine were made. They would*
> *forever be considered among the elite scouts in the game's history.*

Essick would also sign Hall of Famer Tony Lazzeri, who, despite gaudy numbers, was an epileptic, and most scouts stayed away. Not Essick, because he "knew" Lazzeri would be a great player.

In fact, Barrow was right about pretty much everything. Well, maybe he was wrong once or twice.

"[Night baseball] is just a fad," Barrow said when word got out in 1934 that Lee MacPhail's Reds were planning on putting up lights at Crosley Field. "It'll never last after the novelty wears off."

Or when the rumors were running rampant that the flamboyant MacPhail was in talks to buy the Yankees? "Only over my dead body will [Larry] MacPhail buy the Yankees," said Barrow, who, to his dismay, didn't have enough cash to fend off MacPhail's purchase and was kicked upstairs for the final few years of his time with the Yankees.

Others might be surprised that Branch Rickey isn't the pick here. I'll offer that Rickey's best work came when he was in St. Louis.

Yes, he did some great work in Brooklyn, bringing Gil Hodges, Roy Campanella, Duke Snider, Don Newcombe and, of course, Jackie Robinson to Flatbush. That group won pennants in 1947 and 1949, while Rickey was still around. After Rickey lost his battle with Walter O'Malley and left the Dodgers for the Pirates after the 1950 season, "The Boys of Summer" won pennants in 1952, 1953 and 1956, and won it all in 1955.

Impressive, yes, but Rickey's rift with Leo Durocher likely made life a lot harder for Robinson (see chapter 13).

Rickey didn't fight the Durocher suspension that would last the entire 1947 season, and when his old friend Burt Shotton led the Dodgers to the pennant that season, Rickey was more than willing to let Durocher go to the hated New York Giants in the middle of the 1948 season.

But you know, maybe Durocher doesn't blow the 1950 or 1951 pennant race, and maybe, just maybe, he figures out a way to beat the Yankees in 1952 or '53.

The first GM was the best GM: Ed Barrow. *Photo by The Baseball Hall of Fame.*

Also, while Rickey's signing of Robinson broke the color line, it was Rickey's former assistant Buzzie Bavasi who hired Walt Alston, who finally led Brooklyn to a win in 1955.

But don't take our word for it. Ask Rickey himself.

As detailed by Levitt, years after he retired, longtime Barrow rival Branch Rickey was sitting at the same table at a dinner of major-league executives and writers when one of the writers mentioned a compliment Rickey had recently received on his own legendary baseball acumen. Ricky graciously accepted the tribute and then pointed across the table at Barrow.

> *That fellow sitting across the table is the smartest man who ever was in baseball. I will take this glass to prove my point. (Rickey held up an empty champagne glass as a prop.) I adjudge this glass to be perfect in appearance, of excellent material and sound and exquisite construction. Now if I am a connoisseur of glassware, you accept my opinion of it. I am an expert. I have spoken. Now mark the distinction between Mr. Barrow and myself. I have said this is a fine glass. It is Mr. Barrow, however, who would tell you far better than I whether this table, with its silverware, its glasses, its china and its floral decorations, is properly laid out. He knows whether it is balanced or not. That is the difference between Mr. Barrow and myself. That is why I say there has never been a smarter baseball man than Mr. Barrow. He knows what a club needs to achieve balance, what a club needs to become a pennant winner. I, perhaps, can judge the part, but Mr. Barrow can judge the whole.*

Who am I to argue with Mr. Rickey?

19

JOAN PAYSON

All I wanted to do was bring a National League team back to New York.
—*Joan Whitney Payson*

On August 19, 1957, New York Giant owner Horace Stoneham announced that his club, Manhattan's last champions, was giving up its historic Polo Grounds address.

"At a meeting of our board today, they voted permission to transfer the New York Giants franchise to San Francisco," said Stoneham. (Note, he didn't say "we," he said "they.")

"What was the vote?," asked NBC's Gabe Pressman.

"The vote was 8–1," said Stoneham.

"Who voted against it?," followed up Pressman.

"You'll have to ask some of the board of directors, Gabe," said Stoneham.

The lone "no" came from M. Donald Grant, via Joan Whitney Payson, who owned 10 percent of her beloved New York Giants. In a more modern time, the nearly destitute Stoneham might have sold his club to Payson, an independently wealthy collector of Thoroughbreds and fine art. But Stoneham thought San Francisco was going to be the land of milk and honey. (It wasn't for him; he was as bad a businessman in Frisco.)

It was also 1957, and the idea of a woman purchasing a baseball team was pretty unrealistic. But Joan Payson was no ordinary woman, nor was she your run-of-the-mill society multimillionaire. Payson loved baseball and decided if she couldn't buy the Giants, she'd be the person to bring back senior-circuit baseball to Gotham.

Joan Payson, owner. *Illustration by John Pennisi.*

"I don't remember when I first saw the Giants play," said Payson, who was quoted in a *Sports Illustrated* article titled "Happy Blend of Sport and Cash" (May 14, 1962). "My mother used to take me to the Polo Grounds when I was a little girl, and I almost feel as if I'd grown up there. Mother, of course, adored the game. One of my earliest memories are of watching her playing baseball at Palm Beach in the old days."

In 1941, Payson bought a season box at the Polo Grounds, and for the next sixteen years, she was a fixture at Giant games. Later that year, she met Grant, a stockbroker, at a card game, during which they found they shared a love for the baseball Giants. She told Grant she'd love to buy the team, and Grant said he'd love to run it.

Grant was the one to buy a tiny share of the Giants after World War II. Soon after, Payson instructed him to acquire a share for her as well. By 1951, she had invested enough in Giant stock to own nearly 8 percent.

Then came the decision to go west, and while Payson hated the idea, she did fly to San Francisco for the 1958 opener. One place she didn't go was Yankee Stadium, and like more than a few jilted National League fans, she chose to either follow their wayward clubs in the newspapers or to avoid the game entirely.

Then came Bill Shea, who talked his way into convincing old money, and baseball fan Payson, into buying a new team.

Let me interject for a second. I know what you might be thinking. When pitching this book, more than one person questioned my choice for Gotham's best owner. More than one said, "It's her fault we got stuck with M. Donald Grant!"

But while Grant deserves his special place in our Mets Hall of Shame, you simply cannot separate the fact that the team's magical journey from baseball's worst to the Amazin' Mets is part of his résumé. Frankly, if it wasn't for Grant, Payson may have simply stayed a fan rather than an owner.

Also, according to one of my favorite Met books of all time, *The New York Mets: 25 Years of Baseball Magic*, by Jack Lang and Peter Simon, Grant also played a pivotal role in constructing one of the most beloved teams in baseball history.

As the Mets' chairman of the board, Grant knew that the team would need an important figure to run the baseball club. According to Lang and Simon, "Grant wanted Branch Rickey to operate the club but Ricky insisted on a free hand plus several million dollars to develop talent."

However, while Rickey had more than earned the right to have a free hand in running any club, Payson balked at the several million for talent development, especially considering that Rickey's prior arrangements as a GM included a 10 percent commission on every player sale.

When the Yankees "retired" GM George Weiss and manager Casey Stengel, Grant had a new pitch for Payson.

On March 1, 1961, at Grant's suggestion, Payson offered Weiss the position of president of the Mets, which he accepted. He then convinced Payson and Grant to let him hire Stengel. It was Payson who made the call to Stengel.

While the Mets floundered out of the gate, Payson rooted from her seats. Stengel called them "Amazin'," while Weiss bought faded veterans from the old days while he built a farm system from nothing into what all hoped would be a solid foundation.

"I don't think you can calculate what the contributions of Joan Whitney Payson mean to New York and to business overall," said Debra Hazel, a longtime Met fans and public-relations expert.

> *With her lineage and wealth, it would have been more logical for her to grow up with polo ponies, not at the Polo Grounds. Yet she did both. And when New York had no National League franchise, she stepped in and became the first woman to own a baseball team, during the height of the "Mad Men" era. I was a very young girl at the time, but it was incredibly inspiring to see a woman as the president of the organization. Just watching her genuine joy at the games was contagious even through a television screen, and something I think we don't see much of from owners anymore. And I have to believe she would have adored David Wright.*

She sure would have. I suspect, knowing Wright, he would have loved her right back.

Horace Stoneham was thirty-two when he inherited the Giants in 1936 from his father, Charles, a scandal-raising philanderer, gambler and crooked stockbroker. Horace was thirty-two, the youngest owner ever. He was a great fan and, having been groomed for the job, took up his tasks with vim and vigor.

"People have moved out of the city," Stoneham told Robert Creamer for *Sports Illustrated* in the May 20, 1957 issue. "You used to be able—at least over in Brooklyn they could—to go out and get a crowd from within walking distance of the park and fill the stands. You can't do that anymore. Nowadays people have to drive in from the suburbs. We have a transportation problem, and we have a parking problem. It takes people too long to get through the traffic close to the Polo Grounds, and too long to get away."

Had the current Barclays Center been slated for a new Dodgers ballpark, who knows what would have happened? Also, why didn't Robert Moses ever really offer the Shea Stadium project—then the Flushing Meadows Stadium idea—to Stoneham? Maybe it's because Stoneham had decided to move out of New York no matter what.

That's why the narrative of O'Malley convincing Stoneham to move is so tiresome. Maybe he was influential in convincing Stoneham to go all the way to the West Coast, but Stoneham was moving, period. He announced it sooner than O'Malley and had every intention of relocating the Giants to Minneapolis.

History has been kinder to Stoneham, but he really should be held in the same contempt as O'Malley, unless you have read Michael Shapiro's *The Last Good Season*, in which you learn that Robert Moses had as much to do with both team's leaving New York as anyone. Even the excellent *After Many a Summer*, by Robert E. Murphy, which reverts the blame back to O'Malley, makes it clear that Moses had an agenda. Murphy also supports the idea that Stoneham was not duped by anyone.

"O'Malley was still evaluating his prospects in Brooklyn and Queens, and [Stoneham] had a completed deal in place with the City of San Francisco well before the Dodgers had even a tentative arrangement with Los Angeles," wrote Murphy in a June 24, 2007 piece for the *New York Times*, "The Real Villain of New York Baseball."

In the same piece, Murphy states that Stoneham made his decision to move public on August 19, 1957. "If O'Malley had not received, by a margin of one, the vote he needed from the Los Angeles City Council on October 8, 1957, he might have let Stoneham paddle in the Pacific by himself."

Think about that. One vote.

Don't take my word for it. Read both of those books. They are a wonderful way to learn about that era.

One last word about Stoneham comes from Bruce Markusen, who wrote: "Stoneham was not a buffoon. His teams pushed forward the integration movement, while winning a World Series and two National League pennants during the 1950s and '60s. Ahead of his time, he pioneered the movement toward Asian players. Horace Stoneham was far more than Walter O'Malley's sickly little stepbrother."

The crosstown Yankees have more than their fair share of candidates for best owner in Gotham Baseball history.

We'll give the original owners of the Yankees a mention, but little else. Frank J. Farrell and William S. Devery were recruited by American League president Ban Johnson to make sure New York had a franchise in the new league, and so the purchase of the National League's Baltimore Orioles was arranged, and in 1903, the Highlanders were born.

Thankfully, for every Yankee fan since, the two colonels, Jacob Ruppert and Tillinghast L'Hommedieu Huston, bought the Yankees in 1915.

In 1923, the first year of Yankee Stadium, "Colonel" Ruppert bought out Colonel Huston. It was a year in which the Babe Ruth–led Yankees became baseball royalty, winning their third pennant and first World Series. Ruppert was always willing to invest every dollar possible in his club, even when Prohibition was the law of the land and Ruppert's brewery was his main business. At the time of his death in 1939, after ten pennants and seven World Series wins, his loyalty to Miller Huggins as manager, his trust in Ed Barrow to run the club without interference and his construction of Yankee Stadium are all criteria for his being regarded as the best owner of all time. When you also consider that he "understood as a businessman the danger of letting subordinates and outside forces dictate decisions, whether in his brewery or his baseball club," as Steve Steinberg once wrote, the case is even stronger.

Consider that after Ruppert's death, as his estate all but ended the lavish spending—Barrow now had to make the team run on its own steam—the club managed four more pennants and three more World Series championships between 1939 and 1945.

In summary, he was, in many ways, the perfect owner.

Dan Topping, Del Webb and Larry McPhail bought the Yankees from the Ruppert estate in 1945, kicked the great Barrow upstairs and gave the talented but erratic McPhail the reins. In 1947, the Yankees won the first of fifteen American League pennants and ten World Series over a twenty-year period—a remarkable run. It ended with a thud, with the firing of the popular Yogi Berra after winning the 1964 pennant in his first year as manager. The World Series loss to the St. Louis Cardinals resulted in Johnny Keane, the Cards' skipper, turning in his Redbird cap for a navy Yankee one. That was bad enough. Selling the team to CBS was worse, and the team would never recover until Big Stein came to town.

I've already chronicled what George Steinbrenner means to Gotham Baseball in chapter 1, so naming him the best owner would have been logical. But that'd be selfish and inaccurate, as there are too many baseball reasons to do otherwise: the 1982 "Bronx Burners" (though I will always have a soft spot for several players on that team, Dave Collins in particular); his unwillingness to let his "baseball people" run the team, which in many ways is the opposite of Ruppert. But like his dynastic predecessor, Steinbrenner spared no expense on his team, and by the time of his death, he had managed to change the narrative of passive-aggressive lunatic to old lion. His son Hal Steinbrenner has been the best owner in New York sports since taking over the reins.

To me, Nelson Doubleday will always be a savior, taking the ragtag bunch of post-Seaver Mets who played in Grant's Tomb to the highest of baseball heights: the 1986 Mets. But he also allowed himself to be outmaneuvered by Fred Wilpon, who was able to turn his 5 percent share of the Mets to a full partner stake in 1987 (in part because Doubleday's lawyers didn't read the fine print). Wilpon finally bought out the publishing scion in a bitter custody battle in 2002.

The Doubleday Mets were run the way a team should be run: a great GM, a great manager, great players and a payroll befitting a New York National League team.

In my opinion, Doubleday still gets far too little credit for being *the* owner of the Mets during their rise to glory. Part of it was his own doing, as he distrusted the media and granted few interviews during his tenure.

One interview he did give, however, to Nancy Perry of *Fortune Magazine*, was incredibly revealing. Conducted over the course of several conversations with Doubleday in January 1986, months before the amazing summer and fall that was to follow, it is by far the most complete interview ever done with the former Met owner.

I know this chapter is about Mrs. Payson, but let me digress for just a few paragraphs.

Six years ago, he says, everybody thought he was crazy to pay $21 million for a team that had finished last in the National League's Eastern Division for three seasons in a row and was losing money. Friends laughed. Some Doubleday directors questioned his judgment. Worst of all, the "Cuckoo Convoy" thought he was nuts.

Back then Doubleday was in a group of citizens' band [CB] radio freaks who met over the airwaves on their daily commute into Manhattan. A diverse group ranging from a maintenance man to a phone booth manufacturer to a big-time book publisher, they nicknamed themselves the Cuckoo's Nest Convoy. Doubleday's on-air name was the Bookworm. For five years, before CBs gave way to cellular car phones, he and his good buddies met to kibitz, talk sports, and tell jokes. He invited them to lunch at "21," greeted them at Shea Stadium by flashing "Welcome Cuckoos" on the scoreboard, and chattered with them nonstop on the CB.

"It seemed a hideaway for him," says Miles Godin, an advertising executive known to CBers as "Magic Pencil." "At Doubleday, everyone did things because he was Doubleday. But with us he was just the Bookworm."

The day after he bought the Mets, Doubleday stopped as he did every morning for coffee with the Cuckoos at the McDonald's on Astoria Boulevard in Queens. "What are you buying a crummy team like the Mets for?" they razzed him over Egg McMuffins. His reply was prophetic. "Just you wait," he retorted. "Give me five or six years, and they will be a first-place team."

He was right.

But for all of that history, Joan Payson made it possible for me to fall in love with baseball.

I'm not alone in that regard.

It was Payson who started the love affair between those first Met fans—dubbed the "New Breed" by sportswriter Dick Young—and the lovable losers. I hope I am making it clear why I chose her as the best owner of all time. But maybe Joe DeCaro, a true member of the New Breed who runs the popular Met website Metsmerizied.com, has the best take on what Joan Payson meant to the fans.

"It had nothing to do with winning," said DeCaro. "1969 was ecstasy, but no more fun than being at the Polo Grounds down by 10 and yelling 'Let's Go Mets,' cause we were going to put some runs across the plate. Mrs. Payson was the same way. [No matter what the score or the record.] *It was still her team. She owned it but it sure did feel like she was sharing it with all of us. But being there almost every day, rooting her team on, sharing the sorrow of another loss with the rest of us, celebrating the far and few in between triumphs we had (like taking three straight from the Dodgers in the heat of the 1965 pennant race), she was again, one of us. That was because she really did love the Mets."*

BIBLIOGRAPHY

Angell, Roger. *Season Ticket: A Baseball Companion*. Boston: Houghton Mifflin, 1988.

———. *The Summer Game*. New York: Viking, 1972.

Appel, Marty. *Pinstripe Empire: The New York Yankees from Before the Babe to After the Boss*. New York: Bloomsbury USA, 2012.

Bak, Richard. *Cobb Would Have Caught It: The Golden Age of Baseball in Detroit*. Detroit, MI: Wayne State University Press, 1993.

Creamer, Robert. *Babe: The Legend Comes to Life*. New York: Simon & Schuster, 1974.

Devaney, John. *Baseball's Youngest Big Leaguers*. New York: Holt, Rinehart and Winston, 1969.

Dickson, Paul. *Leo Durocher: Baseball's Prodigal Son*. New York: Bloomsbury USA, 2017.

Eig, Jonathan. *Luckiest Man: The Life and Death of Lou Gehrig*. New York: Simon & Schuster, 2005.

———. *Opening Day: The Story of Jackie Robinson's First Season*. New York: Simon & Schuster, 2007.

Golenbock, Peter. *In the Country of Brooklyn*. New York: William Morrow, 2008.

Graham, Frank. *The New York Giants: An Informal History of a Great Baseball Club*. New York: G.P. Putnam and Sons, 1952.

Hirsch, James S. *Willie Mays: The Life, the Legend*. New York: Scribner, 2010.

Irvin, Monte, and James Riley. *Nice Guys Finish First: The Autobiography of Monte Irvin*. New York: Carroll and Graf, 1996.

Jenkinson, Bill. *The Year Babe Ruth Hit 104 Home Runs*. New York: Carroll & Graf, 2007.

Johnson, Davey, and Peter Golenbock. *Bats*. New York: Putnam, 1986.

Kahn, Roger. *The Boys of Summer*. New York: Harper, 1972.

Klima, John. *Willie's Boys: The 1948 Birmingham Black Barons, the Last Negro League World Series, and the Making of a Baseball Legend*. New York: John Wiley & Sons, 2009.

Levitt, Dan. *Ed Barrow: The Bulldog Who Built the Yankees' First Dynasty*. Lincoln: University of Nebraska Press, 2008.

Madden, Bill. *The Pride of October*. New York: Grand Central Publishing, 2004.

Mantle, Mickey, with Mickey Herskowitz. *All My Octobers*. New York: Harper Perennial, 2006.

Mathewson, Christy. *Pitching in a Pinch: Or Baseball from the Inside*. New York: Grosset & Dunlap, 1912.

Montville, Leigh. *The Big Bam: The Life and Times of Babe Ruth*. New York: Doubleday, 2006.

Murphy, Robert. *After Many A Summer*. New York: Union Square Press, 2009.

Nemec, David, and Saul Wisnia. *100 Years of Major League Baseball: American and National Leagues, 1901–2000*. Illustrated edition. Morton Grove, IL: Publications International, 2000.

Nowlin, Bill, and C. Paul Rogers III, eds. *The Team that Time Won't Forget: The 1951 New York Giants*. Phoenix, AZ: Society for American Baseball Research, 2015.

O'Connor, Ian. *The Captain: The Journey of Derek Jeter*. Boston: Houghton Mifflin Harcourt, 2011.

Okrent, Daniel, and Steve Wulf. *Baseball Anecdotes*. New York: Oxford University Press, 1989.

Pietrusza, David. *Judge and Jury: The Life and Times of Judge Kenesaw Mountain Landis*. New York: Diamond Communications, 2001.

Posnanski, Joe. *The Soul of Baseball*. New York: William Morrow, 2007.

Robinson, Jackie, and Alfred Duckett. *I Never Had It Made*. New York: G.P. Putnam's Sons, 1972.

Robinson, Ray. *Greatest World Series Thrillers*. New York: Random House Children's Books, 1970.

———. *Iron Horse: Lou Gehrig in His Time*. New York: W.W. Norton, 2006.

Sandomir, Richard. *The Pride of the Yankees: Lou Gehrig, Gary Cooper, and the Making of a Classic*. New York: Hachette Books, 2017.

Seaver, Tom, with Lee Lowenfish. *The Art of Pitching*. New York: Hearst Books, 1984.

Seib, Philip. *The Player: Christy Mathewson, Baseball, and the American Century*. Cambridge, MA: Da Capo Press, 2003.

Sherman, Joel. *Birth of a Dynasty*. New York: Rodale Books, 2006.

Staples, Bill, and Rich Herschlag. *Before the Glory: 20 Baseball Heroes Talk about Growing up and Turning Hard Times into Home Runs*. Deerfield Beach, FL: Health Communications, 2007.

Torre, Joe, and Henry Dreher. *Joe Torre's Ground Rules for Winners*. New York: Hyperion, 1999.

Vaccaro, Mike. *The First Fall Classic: The Red Sox, the Giants and the Cast of Players, Pugs and Politicos Who Re-Invented the World Series in 1912*. New York: Doubleday, 2009.

Virtue, John. *South of the Color Barrier: How Jorge Pasquel and the Mexican Baseball League Pushed Baseball toward Racial Integration*. Jefferson, NC: McFarland, 2007.

ABOUT THE AUTHOR

Mark C. Healey has been a journalist for over twenty-five years. He is currently the editor-in-chief of *The Wave*, an award-winning newspaper in Rockaway Beach, New York. He lives in New York with his wife, Cailin, and his three children, Julia, Jack and Jessica. This is his first book.

The author, Mark C. Healey, at the 2018 Queens Baseball Convention. *Photo by Matthew M. Lug. Jersey design by Todd Radom. Jersey created by Russ Gompers at Stitches in Whitestone, New York.*